Mark Boyle and members of The Institute of Contemporary Archaeology
'DIG', Shepherd's Bush
**February 1966**

# pocketbooks

Justified Sinners

an archaeology of Scottish counter-culture
(1960–2000)

# Justified Sinners

Edited by
Ross Birrell & Alec Finlay

Contributing Editor
Steve Robb

pocketbooks
Morning Star Publications
Polygon
National Galleries of Scotland
CCA (Glasgow)
Demarco European Art Foundation

2002

Published by:
pocketbooks
Canongate Venture (5), New Street, Edinburgh, EH8 8BH.

Morning Star Publications
Canongate Venture (5), New Street, Edinburgh, EH8 8BH.

National Galleries of Scotland
Belford Rd, Edinburgh, EH4 3DS

Polygon
22 George Square, Edinburgh, EH8 9LF.

Centre for Contemporary Arts,
350 Sauchiehall St, Glasgow, G2 3JD

Demarco European Art Foundation
New Parliament House, 5–7 Regent Road, Edinburgh, EH7 5BL

Typeset in Minion and Univers.
Typesetting and artworking by Cluny Sheeler.
Design concept by Lucy Richards with Alec Finlay.
Printed and bound by Scotprint, Haddington, East Lothian.

Published with the assistance of grants from the Scottish Arts Council National
Lottery Fund and Highlands and Islands Enterprise (HI Arts).

THE SCOTTISH ARTS COUNCIL
National Lottery Fund

Highlands & Islands
ENTERPRISE

A CIP record is available from the British Library.

ISBN 0 7486 6308 8

# List of Contents

# Editor's Acknowledgements

*Justified Sinners*, titled after James Hogg's *Confessions of a Justified Sinner*, is a comradely nod to Douglas Gordon and The Irascibles. It marks out two thematic concerns: firstly, the generative relationship that exists between these artists and curators and the counter-culture of the 1960s and '70s; and secondly, the ebb and flow that characterises the relationship between literature and visual arts.

Conversations with Charles Esche and a character called Pete Horobin, Marshall Anderson and, now, Peter Haining were important influences on this book. The meeting that initiated the anthology was with Ross Birrell, who let slip that he was completing a PhD on anarchism, nihilism and art. This book marries Ross's argument with pocketbooks' integrative approach to contemporary Scottish culture. We each brought partisan approaches to the edit but found few points of disagreement. I thank Ross for the spirit in which he responded to the task.

I also thank the letter writers Edwin Morgan, Halla Beloff, Stephen Willats, Malcolm Dickson, Peter Haining, and Craig Richardson.

The commitment of Steve Robb, archivist for Richard Demarco, enabled us to give a measure of recognition that we felt was entirely Ricky's due. We wish to thank Richard Demarco himself, and also Lorna J. Waite, Alan Jackson, Susan Swan, Toby Webster, Luke Chapman, Chris Atton, Gerry Loose, Morven Gregor, Peter Manson, Graham MacKenzie, Neil Mulholland (ECA), Mel Gooding, Benni Esposito, Ann Simpson, Logan Sisley, Angus Farquhar, Sarah Lownes, Pandy, Sebastian Boyle, Neal Ascherson, Sophy Dale, Eileen Christensen . . . Sinners all!

Thanks are also due to Lucy Richards and the staff of pocketbooks Ken Cockburn, Vicky Hale, Mark Landells and Cluny Sheeler.

A related exhibition, 'A Library for a Justified Sinner' will be held at the Keillor Library, Dean Gallery, Edinburgh, 1st June–8th September 2002.

Alec Finlay

## *from* Wi the Haill Voice

*Weel-respeckit comrades o posterity!*
*Gin yer archaeological scaffies seekin licht*
*on oor benichtit days come scrungein thir clairty*
*petrifacts, ye'll aiblins find me in yer sicht.*
*Wha's yon, ye'll speir. And a boffin'll be bumming*
*abune the bizzin skep o aa yer speirin*
*hoo this was wance 'some bylin-bauldit strummer,*
*hert-seik o aa unbylit watter-farin'.*
*Professor, tak aff thae bicycle-spectacles!*
*I'se shaw ye the age, and gie ye my ain credentials.*

Edwin Morgan
translated from 'Vo Ves' Golos' by Vladimir Mayakovsky

# All Wars Grow Mossy

*Justified Sinners* is a reader of counter-culture in Scotland: of the ephemeral and the sustained; of moments of spontaneous action and organised resistance, refusal and renewal. It is an archaeological dig preceded by an involvement that can be traced back, in the case of Ross, to political activism in his teens, and in my case, to the avant-gardism of my father, Ian Hamilton Finlay, and the 'wars' that he fought – The Fulcrum Dispute, The Little Spartan War, the Follies War, and the bloody War of the Letter. Punk was also a crucial catalyst, as it was for many of the artists and writers included here.

The contributors range from the local to the international; from the wandering Scots who carried the territory of *Scotia Nostra* with them to those welcome visitors from overseas who challenged Scotland's habit of cultural withdrawal.

The term 'archaeology' suggests the process of unearthing: we dug into the ground that lay at our feet, making use of our own bookshelves, those of our friends, and the institutional resources that we could gain access to. The archiving of this period has depended on individuals such as Pete Horobin and Richard Demarco, and organisations such as Counter Information and The Woman's Library.

This book is neither a final record, nor an obituary. While there are aspects of 'document' and 'monument' enshrined here, as a document it is incomplete, and as a monument it is directed towards the time of its making. Although the book is retrospective, an active criticism of contemporary culture is implicit: whither counter-culture now? An undertone emerges from this rough assembly of words and images – a sense of possibility created when a few people shared deep and direct contacts and the demarcation lines between artist and audience were redrawn. This is evident in the Edinburgh Arts Summer Schools, the conversation pieces of Ian Wilson, and in the lectures of Buckminster

Fuller, Beuys and Chomsky. Do our socially engineered schemes of access and participation measure up to these models?

Our archaeology provides a basic framework for an era which so clearly demands further study. There is a pressing demand for new cultural histories of the period – why not a study of the justified sinners of the 1960s, John Calder, Jim Haynes, Alex Trocchi, Edwin Morgan, Mark Boyle, Ian Hamilton Finlay, and Tom McGrath; an analysis of cultural production in Glasgow from Workers City to The Irascibles; an examination of the relationship of the avant-garde to landscape; or a survey of the Demarco era, its origins and achievements? When will Scottish culture be able to sustain a body of criticism worthy of its cultural production?

One of the most interesting aspects to emerge in *Justified Sinners* is the interplay of the traditional or folk elements with those of the international avant-garde – a theme which is reflected in the various representations of the Scottish landscape, a domain of political and environmental struggle, and of mythic renewal. Beuys enacted this as, more recently, has herman de vries. Scots have found it less easy to re-establish this relationship although, in an aside, Tom McGrath has referred to the Highlands as a place of healing where he could renew himself following his involvement with the London scene and heroin. Alastair MacLennan, Angus Farquhar, Ross Sinclair, and Alexander and Susan Maris are just some of the Scottish artists who have responded to the landscape, extending the work of Beuys from a Scottish perspective.

The editorial approach to *Justified Sinners* shifted in response to the impossibility of the task. At one time we planned a detailed chronology. Invitations were sent to a wide range of possible contributors, but we received only one reply (from Neal Ascherson). For a time, the book transformed itself into a visual history (we were entranced by the photographs that Steve Robb was unearthing in the Demarco Archive), but in the end we settled for a chronological, fluid presentation of writing and images.

The book records aspects of cultural production during a period when the traditional divisions between art forms were breaking down. The emphasis is on visual art and literature, though these are more accurately referred to in terms of 'discussion', 'dialogue', 'protest' and 'polemic'. Theatre is absent, though there are a number of actions and happenings that are essentially dramatic. Film also had to be foregone due to lack of space. Amongst many absences, we regret those of John MacGrath and Bill Douglas.

We have not attempted to document political struggles such as the Upper Clyde Shipworkers work-in, the anti-Apartheid movement, Scotland United, Democracy for Scotland, Common Cause, and The anti-Poll Tax campaign. However, we have included particular works that relate to major protest movements – CND and the protest songs of Hamish Henderson and John Mack; Gerry Loose's long poem 'Holy Loch Soap'; and Tom Leonard's 'Shorter Catechism against the Mass Bombing of Iraq and Kuwait'. There are a number of existing histories which cover the politics of this period, though they rarely offer any coverage of the material that is to the fore here.

The anthology reveals the processes by which culture is transformed, and the ways in which cultural production is renewed. We invited seven correspondents to comment on this process, and their letters are a contemporary interpolation into the chronology of the book. The personal nature of their reflections is in sympathy with the 'undertones' that the material reveals.

There will be many readers who disagree with the definition(s) of counter-culture that this book offers. We recognise that the spectrum could have been shifted left, excluding many of the established artists and writers that we have featured.

A question imposes itself: to what degree have the gestures and strategies of counter-culture been assimilated within the mainstream? It may be that an editor constructing an anthology such as this, at any point since 1978, would have felt that they had just witnessed the final act of counter-culture. No one in 1977 wanted to believe that 'God Save the Queen' would become just a song, one that could be re-released for the Queen's Golden Jubilee. The idioms of counter-culture, its stylistic inheritance, have never been so readily available; and yet the magical transformative moments of sharing that are recorded here seem remote, as if concealed by layers of dust. A palimpsest lies buried within these pages, a small ritual object buried somewhere on a remote heathery moor.

Alec Finlay

Poetry reading in The Cellars, Edinburgh by Michael Horowitz.
Present: Alan Jackson, Aurea Lambton, Derry MacDiarmid,
Sue MacDonald Lockhart, Libby Houston, Mal Dean, Paul Pond (Paul Jones).
**1960**

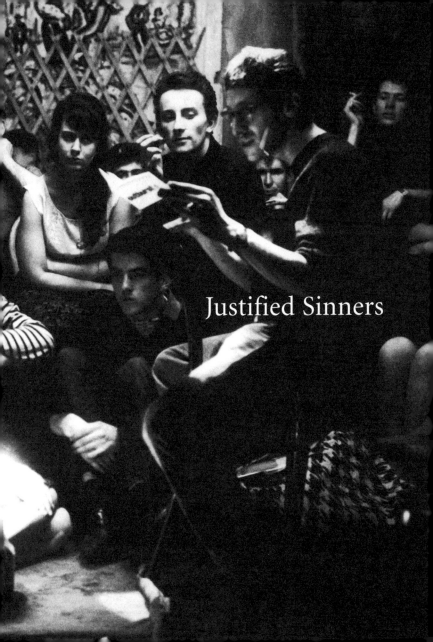

Justified Sinners

# Letter 1

Ross Birrell
Glasgow
January 2002

Dear Reader,

On the way home from a sponsored walk – which had been organised by the Renfrew branch of the Young Socialists to raise funds in support of the miners strike in 1985 – I got talking to a medical student from Paisley. He was in his early twenties, with light red hair and customary cord jacket with leather patches at the elbows. Probably to impress my comrade with my socialist credentials, I mentioned that I had just finished reading *The Ragged Trousered Philanthropists* by Robert Tressell. This is a classic novel that documents the poor working conditions and unemployment endured by a group of painters and decorators in London at the turn of the last century. I was very moved by the book but remember being a little suspicious of Tressell's need to make Barrington a member of the upper classes in disguise, as if to make the class struggle more palatable to the middle class. When we neared his house, the medical student asked if I had read a French novel about the conditions of miners during the nineteenth century. I said I hadn't. He took a small black paperback from a leather satchel and handed it to me. Keep it, he said, turning into his gate. It was Zola's *Germinal*. I was fourteen years old.

The year before going to University was spent in desert boots, rolled-up jeans and a dark raincoat, often travelling in the back of Peter McHugh's car to see bands like the Pastels and The BMX Bandits in venues like Subterraneans in Greenock or the Volcano at Partick Cross. Politics simply melted into the background. I think we all knew that the battle was already lost and no amount of walking in the pissing rain was going to make a blind bit of difference. Years of bitterness ensued, during which I took solace in a cynicism shared by millions. I put my energy into other matters: reading Tom Leonard, listening to the Velvet Underground, The Stooges, Echo and The Bunnymen, Julian Cope,

The Jesus and Mary Chain (thank god for Creation records) and, above all, losing my virginity. Politics did not rear its ugly head again until my first year at Glasgow University when my older brother and I got into an argument with a young railwayman distributing leaflets around the student union on behalf of *Living Marxism*, the magazine of the Revolutionary Communist Party (RCP). The leaflets announced a protest march against grant cuts and the introduction of the student loan scheme. I detested the cuts but was too immersed in defeatism to participate in any march. In defence of our apathy, we claimed that books and pamphlets, such as *Das Kapital* and *The Communist Manifesto*, were just as important as protest marches. He was even living proof of our argument. Of course Marx was also a political organiser and leader of the Workers' International Party, but this fell on deaf ears. Radical politics required heroes, people prepared to sacrifice their lives for the cause. Fuck that. Instead I had anti-heroes: William Blake, Jack Kerouac, William Burroughs, Lou Reed, Iggy Pop, Julian Cope and Friedrich Nietzsche.

As a student I began reading Antonin Artaud and Hugh MacDiarmid. I was drawn to Artaud's frenetic imagination, fuelled by madness and addiction to heroin and to MacDairmid's contradictory blend of firebrand nationalism and trenchant communism. But it was only when I discovered Alexander Trocchi that I knew that I had found an alternative academy. Trocchi's manifestos for a free international university 'The Invisible Insurrection of a Million Minds' and *sigma portfolio* were and remain inspirational texts. And I express my gratitude here to Edwin Morgan for generously photocopying and posting me his collection of Sigma portfolios. They are invaluable documents of the writer as agitator, organiser, and social visionary. It was around this time that, under the influence of alcohol and Artaud,

I wrote my first manifesto. Resigned to the failure of party politics, I was drifting towards anarchism and nihilism – the last refuge from the asphyxiating culture of Thatcher's Britain.

After university, it became almost impossible not to become involved again in political action. Energised by a battle against Landlord-orientated Short Assured Tenancies and inspired by acts of civil disobedience in the widespread resistance to the Poll Tax, I began to seek out books and pamphlets on radical cultural politics. The most important places to find these in Glasgow were Clyde Books, a left-wing bookshop in Parnie Street and, later, the short-lived Fahrenheit 451 in Virginia Galleries. At Clyde Books I found not only the writings of Marx and Engels but also of anarchists such as Bakunin, Goldmann, Kropotkin, Proudhon as well as Noam Chomsky. There were also new titles by AK Press, Rebel Press, Black Flag and Autonomedia. Other anarchist publications like *Counter-Information* you could pick up there or at Transmission Gallery. Perhaps most importantly, I discovered the Situationist International via a small blue pamphlet *On The Poverty of Student Life*. It was also at Clyde Books in 1993 that I picked up a leaflet for an Anarchist Summer School to be held in Govanhill. The summer school was a good experience, seeing old white-haired anarchists battle with Communists, and a precocious young man with swept-back blonde hair and too much make-up storm off after doing battle with a Trot, his long leather coat sweeping round the heels of leather boots. The closing address was by the late Albert Melzer. At the end of the day, I tagged along for a pint with a group of people that included Jim Ferguson and Jim Kelman. I sat in a pub on Victoria Road, sipping my pint with quiet pride at the fringes of the conversation.

The result of the Anarchist Summer School was the (re)formation of the Glasgow Anarchist Group (GAG) which led to the opening of the Solidarity Centre in a lane off Royal Exchange Square. At the same time

I went to join the Free University that met at the Saltoun Arts Project (SAP) in Saltoun Street, but there was only one guy sitting in a cold room, next to a round table splattered with some leaflets. I picked up some flyers, said nothing and left. Sadly, the dedicated left-wing bookshops are now defunct and the only place to stock similar literature today is the Fruitmarket Gallery in Edinburgh.

It was also in 1993 that I started collaborating with Roddy Hunter, writing manifestos and making actions. Roddy was besotted with Artaud, Alastair MacLennan, Joseph Beuys and Tadeusz Kantor, and his performances were heavy with symbolism. For a time Beuys' cross appeared in nearly all our actions. (If you walk down the corridor to the left in the Old Fruitmarket, you can still see the small red crosses I painted on the electrical points on the wall.) With Stuart Buchanan and Alan Benzie (who published *thee data base* and formed the Glasgow Cabal of the Association of Autonomous Astronauts) we got into Stewart Home, Plagiarism and Neoism. The Art Strike 1990–1993 and Home's *Neoist Manifestos* and *The Assault on Culture: utopian currents from Lettrisme to Class War* had become more important to us than four years of university. Immediately, I formed the Dadanarchists and The Society for the Termination of Art.

At this time I was under way with a still unfinished PhD. thesis, *The Theatre of Destruction: Anarchism, Nihilism and the Avant-Garde*, at Glasgow University. In 1996 I invited Gustav Metzger, the inventor of auto-destructive art and originator of the Art Strike 1977–1980, and Stewart Home to participate in a discussion 'Destruction in Art/Destruction of Art' at CCA to mark the thirtieth anniversary of the Destruction in Art Symposium (DIAS). At the same time, following Guy Debord's proposition that 'that which changes our way of seeing the streets is more important than that which changes our way of seeing painting', I began organising 'streetworks', an exhibition of documentation of site-specific live art. It was during the organising of this exhibition at Street Level Gallery that I met Malcolm Dickson. I had attended a benefit gig for *Variant* after it had had its SAC funding cut (a fate which has recently befallen its second incarnation under Billy Clarke and Leigh French) and knew that Malcolm had once been co-editor. I had important discussions with Malcolm regarding the contradictions of counter-culture, public funding of critical art, and the urge to document and preserve the temporary condition of live art. To record these actions seemed to run counter to the very urgency which gave rise to their existence. The contradiction of publicly funding interventionist art tactics became more prevalent in the organising of 'streetworks', as it grew from an exhibition of documentation to a four-day international festival of site-specific live art with artists from Europe, South America, USA and Russia. Was this only officially sanctioned counter-culture, of the kind parodied by the Festival of Plagiarism at Transmission where below the slogan on the invite 'Demolish Serious Culture' was 'Supported by the Scottish Arts Council'? In the end, Strathclyde Police were present at five performances, interrupting three (Julie Laffin, Andre Stitt, Tara Babel) and stopping one (MacLennan's). If nothing else, this testified to the potential of live art interventions to disrupt the attempted smooth running of the regulated city. Nevertheless, by the end of 'streetworks' I was exhausted and vowed never again to undertake such a task fraught with contradictions. That is, until *Justified Sinners*.

Despite its limitations, my hope is that the book will promote debate and discussion. In *Some Recent Attacks: Essays Cultural and Political* (AK Press, 1993) – which I bought in Clyde Books – James Kelman notes 'talk may be cheap, but dialogue is dangerous'. Dangerous because 'it can lead to action'. For me, publishing *Justified Sinners* is a kind of direct action. And it is fitting that is appears at a historical moment when, across the globe, this mode of political action is on the increase. These engaged activists are also 'justified sinners' in search of a better world. In a passage which underpins the philosophy of *Justified Sinners*, Kelman remarks: 'Radical change is always possible. Society can be transformed. This is not the lesson of the 1990s nor is it the lesson of the late 1960s, it is standard information that's been available to humankind for the past couple of millennium.' Let's hope this knowledge remains available long into the next.

Ross Birrell

# The Angries

Great twentieth century: sputnik century:
what an angst is in you, what wide perplexity!
You are a good century and a century of the pit,
cannibal-century to the ideas you beget,
century of the angry young men's target.

Young men get very angry indeed.
Their eyes flash scorn for this period.
They scorn government and they scorn party,
they scorn the church and provisions of philosophy,
they scorn women – and sleep with them,
they scorn the world, its banks and tills,
they scorn, with a painful insight, the ills
that their own miserable scorn leaves them.
The twentieth century is only their stepfather.
The depth of their hate for it, O the depth of it!
The virulently seething teenage fervour
beats dark and thick along the Hudson River;
by Tiber, Seine, and Thames the same teenagers
gather like black dogs come from the same manger.
The sharp, the cross, the sulky, and the weird –
no century has seen their like before.
I see what they don't want – that's clear;
but how to grasp what they are standing for?
It can't – or can it – be a young man's credo
to scold solid and be scolded, nothing more?

Well then, here I am, in the city of Moscow
speaking to them, plainly, as man to man:
what I say is, if I am angry I am
angry only within the love I've fed on,
the love of my own land; loud, but not loud
to hail a poor unbelief. And I am glad
that I can put my trust in the truth of Lenin,
in hammer and ploughshare true to human hand.
If I get angry about this or that –
the anger is within a dignity
of knowing I address friends, knowing I fight
in a front line for a fighter's integrity.
What then is wrong with you? Is it truth you frown for?
'Mass psychosis', the medicos say with a sigh.
All over Europe the boys slouch and glower.
The boys slouch and glower through the U.S.A.

Twentieth century: sputnik century:
tear them out of their thunderous mixed-up scenery!
Give them – no, not a cosy lassitude,
but give them faith in what is right, what is good.
A child is not an enemy. Twentieth century, you
must help them, do you hear? – you help them through!

'Serditye' by Yevgeny Yevtushenko, translated by Edwin Morgan, *Sovpoems*
**1961**

# The Freedom Come All Ye

*to the tune of 'The Bloody Fields of Flanders'*

Roch the wind in the clear day's dawin',
Blaws the cloods heelster gowdie ow'r the bay.
But there's mair nor a roch wind blawin'
Through the great glen o' the warld the day.
It's a thocht that will gar oor rottans
A' they rogues that gang gallus fresh and gay
Tak' the road and seek ither loanins
For their ill ploys tae sport an' play.

Nae mair will the bonnie callants
Mairch tae war, when oor braggarts crously craw,
Nor wee weans frae pit-heid an' clachan
Mourn the ships sailin' doon the Broomielaw.
Broken faimlies in lands we've herriet
Will curse Scotland the Brave nae mair, nae mair;
Black an' white, ane til ither mairriet
Mak' the vile barracks o' their maisters bare.

So come all ye at hame wi' freedom,
Never heed whit the hoodies croak for doom,
In your hoose a' the bairns o' Adam
Can find breid, barley bree an' painted room.
When MacLean meets wi's freens in Springburn
A' the roses an geans will turn tae bloom.
And a black boy frae yont Nyanga
Dings the fell gallows o' the burghers doon.

Hamish Henderson (1919–2002)
The great anthem of the Peace movement, sung at early CND demonstrations at
the Holy Loch.
**1961**

# Ding Dong Dollar

*to the tune of 'Coming Round the Mountain'*

*Oh ye canny spend a dollar when ye're deid*
*Ye canny spend a dollar when ye're deid*
*Singin' ding dong dollar, everybody holler*
*Ye canny spend a dollar when ye're deid*

The Yanks, they dropped anchor in Dunoon
They had a civic welcome frae the toon
As they came up the measured mile, Bonny Mary O' Argyll
Was wearing spangled draws below her goon.

The publicans, they're all daein swell
It's just the thing, it's sure tae ring the bell
All the dollars they will jingle
There'll be no a lassie single
Even though they'll maybe blow us all tae hell.

The Clyde is sure tae prosper now they're here
For they're charging one-and-tenpence for the beer
And when ye want a taxi, they stick it up their – jersey
And charge ye thirty bob tae Sandbank pier.

The Church's Moderator disnae mind
In fact he thinks the Yanks are awfy kind
Fur if it's Heaven that yer going
It's a quicker way than rowing
And there's sure tae be nobody left behind.

John Mack
Pete Seeger gave this song a widespread popularity in the USA.
1961

Dear Yeddie,

From the snows of a Pentland's winter, a visitor to my childhood home; where thirty years ago you sat at the kitchen table drinking strong tea, and watched Dad bend down to set for Albers his saucer of milk. Today the old man sits worn and warm by a little bonfire at the other end of the house. The world outside is blue, chill, perfect; an icy chalice. What has caught in the net since then?

Some of the evidence gathered for our archaeology is set out before me. A faded blue telegram, dated 1962, from the Cuban ambassador to Dad and Jessie, promising poems. I suppose you were to be the translator of that Cuban anthology? I'm trying to remember when the missile crisis was, and I wonder was that the reason for the book? There are some stapled magazines; *Origin* from Kyoto, *Poor.Old.Tired.Horse.* from Gledfield (with a drawing after Malevich on the cover, and your translations of Voznesensky), and folded copies of Hansjorg Mayer's *Futura* broadsheets, in which you and Dad featured. There is a pocket-sized edition of *Sovpoems*, your excavation into the work of Mayakovsky, Khlebnikov, Brecht, Pasternak, and Yevtushenko. Anselm Hollo's *Red Cats* must have appeared around the same time. And finally, there is a yellowing prospectus for Trocchi's *Sigma*.

These fragments and tessarae of the sputnik century are gathered together in an attempt to compose a portrait of an archetypal justified sinner. They read like evidence of a Scottish Spring. Was it a long-awaited thaw? You may even be able to give it a date or describe an event at which that door was flung open. I guess you were already forty years old when *Sovpoems* appeared. (I always remember that story you tell of learning Russian because you fancied another boy in the class). In the Introduction you admit your exasperation with the Modern movement, which in its failure to commit to life 'snaps another link of trust between man and man'. The poems and translations reflect these political and cultural changes, harbingers of the counter-culture portrayed here. The brash voice of angry youth courses through 'The Angries'. I can almost hear your voice, an undertone whispering through the static of time. The poems are also about a new life, a second life.

This credo of youth is engulfed in a chorus of other voices: pilot-plans, social models, manifestos; concrete poetry, sound poetry, Happenings – new models of order in spaces of doubt. But what followed? The epitome of youthful rebellion is a thunderbolt; its aftermath so much charred earth. Re-reading Tom McGrath's *Riverside Interview*, I was struck by the characterisations of Alex Trocchi and R. D. Laing, as justified sinners, strewing psychic chaos, inspiring a thunderous mixed-up scene. Their adventures in consciousness spiralled into drugs, alcoholism, broken relationships and early graves. Tom describes them as prototypes of evil but, while admitting their darkness, pledges himself again to the rebel party.

This schema of the psyche reminded me of my father's description of the Blakean charge that art and conflict hold for him: 'I suppose that what I get at certain moments is a really wild excitement about my work ... if some great clash of ideologies is occurring ... it's like being on the peak of two searchlights that have crossed.' So Yeddie, how do these illuminations and darknesses of the past look to you now?

Best wishes

Eck

Charges to pay

_____s._____d.

RECEIVED

POST

TELE

Prefix.   Time handed in.   O

F    208    2.5

3/19

75

At_____ _____m.

From_____

By_____

MISS JESSIE MCGUFFIE

I  HAVE PHONED CUBA

HAVE POEMS FOR YOUR

ANY DAY THIS WEEK W

DOC

Jessie McGuffie & Ian Hamilton Finlay
Proposed Wild Hawthorn Press selection of Cuban Poetry (unpublished)
**March 1962**

F

a   24   LOPEZ   ++  ‡‡

H.P.Ltd—i068/2

**OFFICE**

**RAM**

Origin and Service Instructions.　Words.

GLASGOW T　35

At ___
To ___
By ___

WEST PARK PLACE
27 MR
62
EDINBURGH

24 FETTES ROW EDINURGH　=

ODAY POETRY IS COMING I

GAZINE CAN YOU COME HERE

UST DISCUSS IT　=

R LOPEZ　++

TELEGRAMS ENQUIRY '' or call, with this form
EH O d by this form, and, if possible, the envelope.

B or

Edwin Morgan
Glasgow
January 2002

Dear Eck,

I well remember that Stonypath visit; I thought it was splendid that someone would call his cat Albers instead of Mog; and I appreciated the strong tea, as I am not an Earl Grey man. Your reminding me of it sparked off a batch of random Sixties recollections. A policeman flashing his torch into an Edinburgh cellar at 2 am to see if anything more improper than a poetry-reading was going on. At a gathering in Tom McGrath's house in Glasgow a joint being passed around, and as it approached me Tom grinned and said 'Moment of truth!', probably expecting I would decline, but I took a good drag and passed it on. Taking poetry to the people in Exchange Square in Glasgow: moderately successful? – with no microphone and against a strong wind and a few boozy interruptions. During the truly scary Cuban Missile Crisis of October 1962, wondering if as an army veteran I would be called up again, and if so, what could I do, or would it be too late to do anything? Joining the Bachelor Clan, one of the earliest semi-public gay organisations in Scotland, and having a partner who went wild on poppers – oh those times!

But to give more than a brief flavour, I would have to say that the whole decade for me was a period of liberation. I would almost date my life from 1960 instead of 1920. I was productive in poetry; I was in love; I was fascinated by space exploration; popular music came of age and was a huge delight; films (film has always meant a lot to me) – *La Dolce Vita*, *L'Avventura*, *Andrei Rublyov*, *2001*, *The Gospel According to St Matthew*, *The Colour of Pomegranates* – burst across the imagination; and even an enormous negative like the Vietnam War (which seemed to go on for ever) released such powerful jets of human concern that it made the decade an unforgettable gouge on the parchment.

Yes, I go along with the idea of a Scottish Spring. It was genuinely a time of beginnings, a time of openings, and I always felt that those who left Scotland then – e.g. Kenneth White, Douglas Dunn – were too impatient and should have stayed. New international configurations – Scottish–American, Scottish–Russian, Scottish–Brazilian – appeared. New genres like concrete poetry and sound-poetry challenged a fair amount of opposition. I remember Hugh MacDiarmid growling in 1970: "I'd hate an Ian Finlay poem on my gravestone." Publishers like Wild Hawthorn, Migrant, Eugen Gomringer, Hansjörg Mayer, encouraged Scotland to see the world and the world to see Scotland. My *Sovpoems* (1961) paid tribute to Russian writers from Mayakovsky to Yevtushenko, and my *Starryveldt* (1965) was in a sense a defence of concrete poetry, showing it at work on themes of politics and science as well as on semantic reconstruction and linguistic play. At the same time I was writing poems about Glasgow which an ongoing drama of social and architectural change virtually demanded. I did not see anything paradoxical in pursuing these varied poetries. I was not bound by dogma. I wrote what I wanted to write. I knew the time was ripe to do new things. Unconventional sinners – I was one myself – haunted 'Glasgow Green', and were they justified? If they were, even to the slightest degree, then that poem was a breakthrough. You will gather that I was more Times Square than wild hawthorn. I was more in tune with Ginsberg's *Howl* and *Kaddish* and the Kerouac of *October in the Railroad Earth* than with the Black Mountain poets favoured by your dad and Gael Turnbull. It did not matter. Both groups of American writers were needed. We had a double benefit.

You mention R. D. Laing and Alex Trocchi. Laing I didn't know, but I knew Trocchi quite well. He fits your title very neatly, as apart from biography he nods back in several of his books to the Hogg of *Confessions of a Justified Sinner*. I remember him first of all as a student at Glasgow University at the time when I was a young lecturer in the English

Department. What was he? Brilliant, wayward, charming, alarming, passing exams on Benzedrine, starting up a pig farm shortly before his finals. Everyone knew he would make his mark sometime, somehow, somewhere. *Young Adam* (1954) and *Cain's Book* (1960) are still read and are still going to be read. His public spat with MacDiarmid at the 1962 Writers Conference in Edinburgh is part of the whole mythology of the Sixties, and was an unplanned happening not unlike the planned 'happenings' of the time, but it was also a defining moment in Scottish culture, peculiarly galling to MacDiarmid whose *Collected Poems* had just been published after years of neglect: a new era was in fact breaking out of the closet. I shared the table (and microphone and whisky) with Alex at that meeting, and remember it vividly. I didn't see him frequently thereafter, but we kept in touch, and I was one of the five Scottish recipients of his 30-odd *Sigma Portfolios* (1964–1967) – the others being Hugh MacDiarmid, Tom McGrath, Kenneth White, and your dad. This 'invisible insurrection of a million minds', as the portfolios were planned to be, cheaply cyclostyled and now a rarity on the market, comes across as the paradigmatic Sixties phenomenon, with its emphasis on revolt, liberation, alternative lifestyles, anti-universities, and worldwide cultural networking. Was all this swept away? Not quite. These are strange half-derelict sites, which are today re-visited and re-discussed. I can see Alex cocking a quizzical eyebrow and looking down his long nose at those who talk of his 'failure', his few novels, the silence of his later years. He sometimes looked devilish, and there are some who thought he *was* devilish. I don't know. I retain a certain affection for him, probably because I knew him when I was young. I acknowledge him as a Glaswegian risk-taker. He ripped the tent-flap apart – I don't want to see it – oh yes you do – look – look –

Edwin Morgan

# Festivals & Happenings

I went to a Conference on the Novel in the middle of August – a fantastic affair; did you read anything about it? ... People jumping up to confess they were homosexuals or heterosexuals; a Registered Heroin Addict leading the young Scottish opposition to the literary tyranny of the Communist Hugh MacDiarmid ... the Yugoslav group in schism and their ambassador threatening to pull the Belgrade Opera and Ballet out of the Festival because the non-official delegate had been allowed to speak before the official delegate; an Englishwoman novelist describing her communications with her dead daughter; a Dutch homosexual, former male nurse, now a Catholic convert, seeking someone to baptise him; a bearded Sikh with hair down to his waist declaring on the platform that homosexuals were incapable of love, just as he said hermaphrodites were incapable of orgasm (Stephen Spender, in the chair, murmured that he should have thought they could have two). And all of this before an audience of over two thousand per day, mostly, I suppose, Scottish Presbyterians. The most striking fact was the number of lunatics both on the platform and in the public. One young woman novelist was released temporarily from a mental hospital in order to attend the Conference, and she was one of the milder cases. I confess I enjoyed it enormously ...

Mary McCarthy
extract from letter to Hannah Arendt
**28 September 1962**

In 1962 the Director of the Edinburgh Festival, Lord Harewood, invited John Calder and Jim Haynes to organise a Writers Festival. Erich Fried, William Burroughs, Norman Mailer, Colin MacInnes, Henry Miller, and Angus Wilson attended and events included the spat between Hugh MacDiarmid and Alex Trocchi. The 1963 Drama Conference featured the 'Happenings' by Allan Kaprow, Mark Boyle, Ken Dewey and Charles Lawson, including the notorious 'naked lady' episode.

# Edinburgh Happenings

After the event, it became fashionable to dismiss the entire Edinburgh Drama Conference in one of two ways. If you were a philistine (e.g. Scots) and disliked nudes with your theories, you would knock its vulgarity and lack of seriousness. If you were an 'intellectual', you sneered because it didn't unearth new concepts or maintain the level of Socratic discourse. Gradually one became aware of the low, throbbing sound of an organ and an electronic tape feeding back carefully edited excerpts from the week's discussions. Then a nude on a trolley was pulled across the balcony above the speaker's platform. Carroll Baker, who had been seated on the platform, took this as her cue to descend and begin clambering over the seats as if hypnotized by Allan Kaprow ... By this time a group of strangers had appeared at the windows overhead hollering: 'Me; Can you see me!' – and a mother ushered a baby across the stage pointing out the celebrities in the crowd. The final beat was when the curtains behind the speaker's platform suddenly tumbled down to reveal rows of shelves containing over a hundred sculpted heads illuminated by footlights. The actions had intended to disperse attention and create a number of different areas of interest, and by this time, they had fully succeeded. No one knew precisely what was happening nor where.

The event, conceived and directed by Ken Dewey, became the subject of the afternoon's debate. For the first time since it had begun, that staid old conference with its dour Scottish squares and frumpy *litterateurs* was bristling with feeling. The majority, led by an incensed Ken Tynan (hurling words like 'totalitarian' and 'apocalyptic'), deplored the interruption ... Alexander Trocchi spat the word 'Dada' back into Tynan's face and exclaimed that the critics could not simply explain away new forces in art by bundling them into ready-made classifications.

Charles Marowitz, from *New Writers 4*, Calder & Boyars
1963

# Event for Judge, Jury and Prisoner at the Bar

1. The prisoner enters the witness box to give evidence.

2. He swears to tell the truth, the whole truth and nothing but the truth!

3. He makes a serious and profound attempt to tell the whole truth.[1,2]

1. Various objections will undoubtedly be raised – it will be pointed out that the words 'the whole truth' are legally defined as meaning the whole truth relevant to the case at issue. But this is answered by pointing out that whereas the court are at liberty to define and control all other areas of court procedure, this one area according to their ethic, is a contract between the subject and God and their definitions and limitations are meaningless. Besides all truth is relevant to any case at issue.

2. The event was prepared in the aftermath of BIG ED, the Edinburgh event in which Mark Boyle collaborated with Ken Dewey and Charles Lawson. A girl who had appeared naked in the event was prosecuted and the police told Dewey and Boyle that if they got a conviction against the girl they would do them next. In the event an Edinburgh magistrate came out with a resounding judgement in the girl's favour, accusing the press of hypocrisy. So the event for *Judge, Jury and Prisoner at the Bar* was never performed.

Mark Boyle
From *Journey to the Surface of the Earth, Mark Boyle's Atlas and Manual* (1970)
**1963**

# R.D. Laing

# the divided self

First published by Tavistock Publications
**1960**

# CAIN'S BOOK
## Alexander Trocchi

**Jupiter Books**

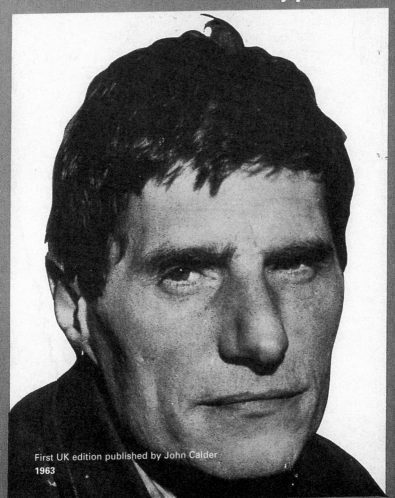

First UK edition published by John Calder
1963

I say it is impertinent, insolent, and presumptuous of any person or group of persons to impose their unexamined moral prohibitions upon me, that is dangerous both to me and, although they are unaware of it, to the imposers, that in every instance in which such prohibition becomes crystallized in law an alarming precedent is created. History is studded with examples, the sweet leper stifled by the moral prejudice of his age. Vigilance. Dispute legal precedent.

In my study of drugs (I don't pretend for a moment that my sole interest in drugs is to study their effects … To be familiar with this experience, to be able to attain, by whatever means, the serenity of a vantage point 'beyond' death, to have such a critical technique at one's disposal – let me say simply that on my ability to attain that vantage point my own sanity has from time to time depended) – in my study of drugs I have been forced to run grave risks, and I have been stymied constantly by the barbarous laws under which their usage is controlled. These crude laws and social hysteria of which they are a symptom have from day to day placed me at the edge of the gallow's leap. *I demand that these laws be changed.*

The hysterical gymnastics of governments confronting the problem of the atomic bomb is duplicated exactly in their confrontation of heroin. Heroin, a highly valuable drug, as democratic statistics testify, comes in for all the shit-slinging. Perhaps that is why junkies, many of whom possess the humour of detachment, sometimes call it 'shit'.

We cannot afford to leave the potential power of drugs in the hands of a few government 'experts', whatever they call themselves. Critical knowledge we must keep vigilantly in the public domain. A cursory glance at history should caution us thus. I would recommend on grounds of public safety that heroin (and all other known drugs) be placed with lucid literature pertaining to its use and abuse on the counters of all chemists (to think that a man should be allowed a gun and not a drug!) and sold openly to anyone over twenty-one. This is the only safe method of controlling the use of drugs. At the moment we are encouraging ignorance, legislating to keep crime in existence, and preparing the way for one of the most heinous usurpations of power of all times ... all over the world ...

*

For a long time I have suspected there is no way out. I can do nothing I am not. I have been living destructively towards the writer in me for some time, guiltily conscious of doing so all along, cf. the critical justification in terms of the objective death of an historical tradition: a decadent at a tremendous turning point in history, constitutionally incapable of turning with it as a writer, I am living my personal Dada. In all of this there is a terrible emotional smear. The steel of the logic has daily to be strengthened to contain the volcanic element within. It grows daily more hard to contain. I am a kind of bomb.

Alexander Trocchi<br>**1963**

Established in 1949, John Calder's Press published Samuel Beckett in the 1950s, and (as Calder & Boyars) influential texts of sixties counter-culture by William Burroughs, Henry Miller, John Cage and Hubert Selby Jnr.

# *from* Invisible Insurrection of a Million Minds

Revolt is understandably unpopular. As soon as it is defined it has provoked the measures for its containment. The prudent man will avoid his definition which is in effect his death-sentence. Besides, it is a limit.

We are concerned not with the *coup-d'état* of Trotsky and Lenin, but with the *coup-du-monde*, a transition, a transition of necessity more complex, more diffuse than the other, and so more gradual, less spectacular. Our methods will vary with the empirical facts pertaining here and now, there and then.

Political revolt is and must be ineffectual precisely because it must come to grips at the prevailing level of political process. Beyond the backwaters of civilisation it is an anachronism. Meanwhile, with the world at the edge of extinction, we cannot afford to wait for the mass. Nor to brawl with it.

The *coup-du-monde* must be in a broad sense cultural ... The cultural revolt is the necessary underpinning, the passionate substructure of a new order of things.

What is to be seized has no physical dimensions nor relevant temporal colour. It is not an arsenal, nor a capital city, nor an island, nor an isthmus visible from a peak in Darien. Finally, it is all these things too, of course, all that there is, but only by the way, and inevitably. What is to be seized – and I address that one million (say) here and there who are capable of perceiving at once just what it is I am about, a million potential 'technicians' – is ourselves. What must occur, now, today, tomorrow, in those widely dispersed but vital centres of experience, is a revelation. At the present time, in what is often thought of as the age of mass, we tend to fall into the habit of regarding history and evolution as something the goes relentlessly on, quite outwith our control. The individual has a profound sense of his own impotence as he realises the immensity of the forces involved. We, the creative ones everywhere, must discard this paralytic posture and seize control of the human process by assuming control of ourselves. We must reject the conventional fiction of 'unchanging human nature.' There is in fact no such permanence anywhere. There is only becoming.

Organisation, control, revolution: each of the million individuals to whom I speak will be wary of such concepts, will find it all but impossible with a quiet conscience to identify himself with any group whatsoever, no matter what it calls itself. That is as it should be. But it is at the same time the reason for the impotence of intelligence everywhere in the face of events, for which no one in particular can be said to be responsible, a yawning tide of bloody disasters, the natural outcome of that complex of processes, for the most part unconscious and uncontrolled, which constitute the history of man. Without organisation concerted action is impossible; the energy of individuals and small groups is dissipated in a hundred and one unconnected acts of protest ... a manifesto here, a hunger strike there. Such protests, moreover, are commonly based on the assumption that social behaviour is intelligent; the hallmark of their futility. If change is to be purposive, men must somehow function together in the social situation. And it is our contention that there already exists a nucleus of men who, if they will set themselves gradually and tentatively to the task, are capable of imposing a new and seminal idea: the world wait for them to show their hand.

Alexander Trocchi
**1963**

First published in *New Saltire Review*. Trocchi distributed *sigma portfolio* between 1964 and 1967: 'an entirely new dimension in publishing, through which the writer reaches his public immediately ... and by means of which the reader gets it, so to speak, "hot" from the writer's pen.' (AT)

## *from* Letters from Gourgounel

In the *Will to Power*, Nietzsche speaks of the most crying need of our civilisation: 'temporary isolation … a kind of deepest concentration on oneself and self-recovery – not to avoid temptations, but obligations.' It is the need to get away from politics, nationality, education, newspapers – 'away from the tyranny of stimuli and influences which sentence us to spend our strength in reactions, and does not permit us any more to let it *accumulate* to the point of *spontaneous activity*.'

After five years at university (with a break of isolation in between, at Munich) I left Britain where I felt I was bound to live more and more by reaction only, and went to Paris. But after two years in that city, I found reaction against setting in, and removed a few miles out of it to the relative quietude of Meudon, where I lived in a house surrounded by a garden of pear trees, apple trees, plum trees, peach trees, cherry trees, and began to feel and live and express the kind of life I wanted.

In the same year that I removed out of Paris (a *chambre de bonne* on the seventh floor, Avenue de Saxe) to Meudon (a room in that villa), I went on a spring trip to the South. I'd heard that houses could be had for a song in the Ardèche, and had got together some extra cash by doing translations and several other odd jobs. I left from the Gare de Lyon and arrived one April morning in Montelimar. There I hired a bicycle for one franc fifty a day (a new tyre thrown in) and got out on the road . . .

Well, I'd travelled around quite a bit, I'd met and talked with a lot of people, but I still hadn't found the place I was looking for, that essential place I imagined, full of solitude, silence, wind, sun and storms. But on the tenth day, I came upon Gourgounel, an abandoned farm in the valley of the Beaume . . .

'They ask me why I live in the blue mountains. I smile without answering', says Li Po. Well, let me try to give some kind of answer.

I've come to this place to undertake some personal alchemy. The idea is to set a whole mass of matter: knowledge, imaginings, feelings – all the accumulations of the past ten years or so, to the process of fire (Ardèche, etymologically, means 'burning country'), and see what comes out of it. Maybe not more than one of those little 'sparks' Meister Eckhart speaks of, but that will at least be *something*. Whereas in the city, everything was just going round and round in sickening confusion. In this context, I was beginning to feel as lonely as a rhinoceros, separated from myself as much as from others. Whereas here, in this solitude, I'm not lonely at all. Because here I can get absorbed in the work.

So, I've come here, not for some pastoral regression, but in order to get on with a certain kind of work. The sixteenth-century German alchemist, Kunrath, puts it this way: 'Study, meditate, sweat and work, and a healthful flood will come to you from the great world, waters that are the true and natural water-of-life.'

I'd like it to be said of this book what Chen says of his book of Vajrayana meditations: 'People have described it as a very fragrant work since at the time of reading it they noticed a sweet smell in the room . . .'

Kenneth White
**1966**

From 1961 to 1975 White lived at Gourgounel, France, mostly springs and summers. The first summer gave life to his first book, *Letters from Gourgounel*.

# Letters to Ernst Jandl

Ian Hamilton Finlay
Edinburgh
1964

Dear Ernst,

I began by writing short stories, then little dramas, which were sometimes broadcast, and only began writing poems some five or six years ago. This soon brought me into conflict with the other Scottish poets, and though I am close friends with Augusto de Campos, in Brazil, and with some American poets (such as Robert Creeley, do you know his work?), and a few people in England ... I have always been very isolated here.

*

It is difficult to use Scottish words in concrete poems, because they often seem out of place. We have a whole school of poets here who write in Scots, but they use only old-fashioned forms, and their language too is from earlier centuries, and not the Scots that is still spoken. I also wrote a little book [*Glasgow Beasts, an a Burd*] ... entirely in the Glasgow dialect, which is considered very improper, and uncouth ... The book ... caused a great scandal, and was attacked by all the Scottish poets. A whole pamphlet, about fifty times its size, was written about it by an older Scottish poet [Hugh MacDiarmid, *The Ugly Birds Without Wings*]. The poems sold (out) four editions in a year, and though it is long out of print, people write almost every week asking for it. It was a very extraordinary episode ... I invented, in view of all the attacks on us, a Protest march (which was entirely mythological), and a special law was made by the Edinburgh Magistrates to ban this. It was even reported on the radio that we had a zeppelin, which was going to bombard the Edinburgh Festival. So powerful is myth!

*

I am thinking of making a little toy theatre. Only it would be very old-fashioned, if I did make it ... I hate audience participation theatre. Do you? I think it is rude to involve people, it is like attacking them. Once, in the Festival here, a lady in the front row in a theatre-in-the-round production offered the leading actress a chocolate, and I thought that was very just: involvement should work both ways, if it is going to be insisted on ...

I am busy digging a small Sunken Garden, which is to have walls covered with rock-plants, a little lawn of camomile, and three poems of 'one-word', carved on stones (by a sculptor). So you see, I am becoming an unskilled AVANT-GARDEner. [I would like] your permission to use the few sentences from your essay on sound poetry (in *Form*), in my little booklet. You may remember that I mentioned it before, and I did not then think of asking permission because I was viewing the wee booklet as a collage/montage, in which the quoted text did not mean in the booklet what it meant in the essay. So I no more thought of asking permission than I imagine Schwitters thought of asking the Bus Company for permission to 'quote' a bus-ticket in a collage painting. But Phil Steadman thinks I should ask, so of course I hasten to do so, for I wouldn't want to be presuming or rude. Another difficulty is that I can't 'explain' the booklet – I am in the position of a shopkeeper who, on the phone, yesterday, was trying to explain to me how to set a mole-trap, which looked like a Chinese puzzle. However, Phil has set me worrying and I am wondering if I ought, too, to write to the skippers of all the boats (fishing boats) which I quote from – A; PD; BCK; etc. (The little sound-poems they wear on their sails and bows.) Ah dearie me, who would be a poet? Life is full of problems.

Love, Aye
Ian

Ian Hamilton Finlay
1964–67

Ernst Jandl, Austrian poet and avant-gardist. The letters date from the period of Finlay's involvement (along with Edwin Morgan) in the Concrete Poetry International and his move out of the city to begin work on the garden at Stonypath (later Little Sparta). The 'wee booklet' referred to is *Ocean Stripe 5* (see over).

*Sound poetry is a montage
of vocal sounds, achieved
through mechanical means.
The montage consists of
the making and structuring
of sounds and echoes, through
phonemes, letters, syllables,
words, and through physical
modulations of all these.*

Ian Hamilton Finlay
from *Ocean Stripe 5*
1967

*The basic material is not
the word but the letter.*

Alan Riddell, from *Eclipse: Concrete Poems 1963–71*

# Starryveldt

starryveldt
 slave
southvenus
 serve
SHARPEVILLE
 shove
shriekvolley
 swerve
shootvillage
 save
spoorvengeance
 stave
strikevault
 strive
subvert
 starve
smashverwoerd
 strive
scattervoortrekker
 starve
spadevow
 strive
sunvast
 starve
survive
 strive
so: VAEVICTIS

Edwin Morgan
from *Starryveldt*, Morgan's first collection of concrete poetry
**1965**

Ivor Davies
**September 1966**

Controlled explosion at the Army Drill Hall, Edinburgh. In association with the 'Destruction in Art Symposium' (DIAS) organised by Gustav Metzger and John Sharkey, held in London.

# Personal Statement

The function of art
Is the corruption of
the human spirit.

I will make your children
drug addicts and perverts.
I will disease their flesh
and fracture their minds,
irreparably.

They will search for the heroic
and grow sick at trivia.
Confused and hesitant, they will regard
a thousand aesthetic monuments,
unable to decide.
And while they wonder,
the animals will take their daughters.

Their flesh will become parchment.
And I will drain away their souls.

Tom McGrath
**1973**

# *from* The Riverside Interviews

There was a directness of vision that they seemed to have ... in Laing's case, madness, in Burroughs' case, paranoia, and in Trocchi's case heroin. The fact was they had this thing I wanted, this kind of manhood vision ... that they were real ... To an extent, Laing was a guru ... But the scene was so hyped that it got too much to take ...

There was a kind of tyranny about the activities of those who were later regarded as the gurus of the Underground. On the other hand, it was exciting to see people shaping another reality. The Albert Hall reading rather sums up that mid-sixties exuberance and decadence. The energy of Trocchi and those around him released a tide of mass communication that you normally associate with football crowds. It brought poetry closer to drama ... A lot of different streams of dissent and alternative living were brought together. Yet the junk habit was so entrenched, behind the glamour. I remember Christopher Logue walking out on Trocchi that day because Trocchi insisted on having a fix. He said, "Alex, if you're going to do that, I'm leaving," and he stormed out ... Corso, Trocchi, and others were behaving as if the event could only exist on those terms. Neither myself nor Davy Graham – the guitarist – were doing it at that time. We went outside and played football in the street ...

There was another stream: non-violence. I was heavily influenced by Theodore Roszak, who edited *Peace News*. Through that magazine I read Thomas Merton, Kenneth Rexroth, anarchists like Paul Goodman and [Alex] Comfort, and many of the Civil Rights people in the states. *Liberation* magazine also influenced me. That was coming in from one side into *International Times*, but it was too moral for me – and it still is. Although the peace and love is an aspect of me, I thought I'd like to go with the sinners: people like Laing and Trocchi ...

Tom McGrath
*The Riverside Interviews: 6*
**1983**

# Total Psychic Orgasm

It had all started peacefully enough. Tom and his friends on the floor, cross-legged, chanting OMMMM ... Jazzmen and audience feeling a bit spare. What we should have, he then said, was a kind of ritual. And we're going to start by everybody putting a pound on these trays. Then I'm going to burn them. Chuckle. General disbelief. Actually, no one stumped up anything more precious than a few old tickets to the Trav. What did he expect? Hard to say what the chuckle said. Then the performance started, gently, gently, till WHOOOOSH! He was off ... shouts, raspberries, howls blasting through the mike, the horns and drums, brass and whistles reaching an incredible pitch. The audience looking at their feet, or holding their ears, or faces like masks – completely thrown. Then all back to gentleness. Cross-legged. He got up and wandered around like nothing had begun and nothing ended. Someone else had to say that was it. The whole man, face, body and voice had gone through transformations. During the performance the body had seemed like a baby's then again like your mum's or aunty's, fat and mammary, or hard and threatening and masculine. It was like he was getting together for himself some sense of intra-sexual evolution and crisis. And the odd thing was how he could look and sound, at beginning and end, like some young Glasgow bloke who'd somehow been persuaded to join in some Buddhist and freaky session. I got the feeling that that young bloke, unassuming and diffident without being exactly embarrassed, was a sort of proto-Tom McGrath, the basic key on which he played his whole theme and variations of traumas and hang-ups and identities which he exorcises and celebrates. And that it is in such moments of exorcism and celebration that Tom McGrath feels fully alive. A kind of total psychic orgasm takes place, all the better the more participate in it.

From profile of Tom McGrath in *Scottish International*
**1972**

# A Scotch Poet Speaks

Och, I wish you hadn't come right now;
You've put me off my balance.
I was just translating my last wee poem
Into the dear old Lallans.

Alan Jackson
1967


# Scotland the Wee

Scotland the wee, creche of the soul,
of thee I sing

land of the millionaire draper, whisky vomit
and the Hillman Imp

staked out with church halls, gaelic sangs
and the pan loaf

eventide home for teachers and christians,
nirvana of the keelie imagination

Stenhousemuir, Glenrothes, Auchterarder, Renton
– one way street to the coup of the mind.

Tom Buchan
1966

# Letter from a Partisan

Up here in the orgone stream our muscular
armour relaxes com-
pletely, pinetrees shimmy
like dildos on their moist pelvic
floor and oxygenated water
cascades past our sensitised ears.

In our mountain command post
our synapses are in full spasm suffused
with invisible telepathic
vibrations as we plan the liberation of Scotland
from the puritanical conformist unionist hordes.

Our cap-
tain (confined to his sleeping-bag
with a painful bout of genital
cramp) issues his orders in curt quiet tones:
you can hear the copper clunk of bullets, the plop
of rain on a mapcase.

Message boys slip away through the bracken
to contact our suburban groupuscules: they
travel on foot hitching occasional lifts
from unsuspecting lairds and suspicious ministers
stopping only at lonely Highland mo-
tels for a lay and a sip of the cratur.

At the head of the Black
Loch we ambush a file of artificial insemination
technologists. We entertain com-
rades from Truro – for them
our uniformed girls open their soft
parts as a gesture of international solidarity. We question an agent
provocateur from St Andrews House nearly
yanking his balls off. It's a hard
life  but a good one
up here in the mountains. Tell Charlie
thanks for the truss. Scotland forever!

Tom Buchan

**1969**

*from* Journey to the Surface of the Earth

And during the exhibition at the Institute of Contemporary Arts in London [1969] you blindfold the public soon after they come in, and you put a gun in their hands, and you lead them and you point the gun more or less in the direction of the unknown target, and they fire this dart and they take off the blindfold, and they realise they've fired at this huge map of the world, and you have quickly discovered it's almost no good trying to offer explanations, that the day of explanations is over ... The problem is to select from an almost infinite spectrum of reasons why ... and Christopher comes in and says "I can't understand why you're so hung up with the idea of objectivity. Objectivity is motiveless appraisal, and I can't see how any appraisal can be motiveless" ... later that evening the police come round to collect Christopher because he is supposed to be mad and he's just escaped from his asylum they put him in two days ago, and Christopher jumps through the glass of the third floor window at the back, and when you get round there, for one marvellous moment, you think he's made it, and there's this image of him vaulting over the wall in the moonlight, and then you see his feet sticking up out of the area and while you're holding him and feeling the warm blood soaking his clothes, and you're crying and loving him, and sure he's dying, and your thighs are all sticky with his blood, and he comes round for a moment and starts to apologise for breaking the window, and says he just wanted to be free. And you can't even begin to explain to him or yourself, and you weren't even able to explain adequately to the judge that sent him there in the first place, why he should be free, and why he didn't want to have them with their drugs and their electric shock treatment buggering around with his ideas even if they are hallucinations.

And you think about Mike Rathledge and Robert and Kevin and Hugh and working with the Soft Machine and their shattering, acetylene music and how can anyone hear it live then ask for explanations.

How could anyone go to Beethoven and say "Why?" How can you go to a girl with her baby and say "Why?" But they do ... And in the end all you can say is, "I know what I'm on about", and Joan knows what she's on about, and Johnny and Des know what they are on about and we're going to do this journey, making multi-sensual presentations of 1,000 random sites across the surface of the earth ... World Series. We had a fierce urge to make one of the two World sites in Scotland. It's strange that in spite of all your efforts to be a cynical émigré you can't ever get away from the pull of your own country. I mean I have tried with enormous commitment (it's really fundamental to our whole approach to the world) to be as objective as possible and to prise open the grip of the prejudices and preferences induced by my hereditary and upbringing. In spite of it all, Scotland still seems to be my ideal of how a country should be. It's the right kind of size, the people have the right kind of conceit of themselves. They actually enjoy one another's company fiercely. Race doesn't enter into it. I've known Scottish people who are Jewish, West Indian, Italian and Pakistani. They all seem to take on with amazing speed and never lose the condition of being Scots. Glasgow seems to me to be the archetypal City. Its streets are dark gorges with seething currents. It's a green and grey and black city. But my memories of it are all in the most lurid Technicolor. A million vivid memories from the Barrowland Ballroom to the Barracuda Bar. I'm away from it all now like millions of others and all I have left is a deep longing. But I can't think of a Scot I've ever met that I wouldn't trust my life to. It's as though in that city people feel that they see the weal and woe of the world, they try everything from cynicism to despair and decide in the end, that the only answer is a kind of fierce joy.

Mark Boyle

## *from* King for a Day

1. King for a day piece.
2. Wear a hat with a silver lining piece.
3. Fools rush in and make new Art, piece.
4. Art is a many splendoured thing.
5. McLean and the nude, work.
6. McLean and the Still-life piece.
7. McLean and the portrait piece.
8. McLean and the landscape, lakescape, piece.
9. Take a line for a walk piece.
10. Piece for a specific part of the body piece.
11. Head work.
12. Foot work.
13. Leg work.
14. Arm work.
15. Mouth work.
16. Caro revisited work.
17. King revisited work.
18. Tucker revisited work.
19. A fresh look at Henry Moore (piece).
20. Impression work.
21. Face pieces (smiling) piece.
22. Face piece (smiling laughing simultaneously) piece.
23. Multi-facial expression work.
24. Put yourself in my place piece.
25. Joke piece (visuals sounds) multi/mixed media.

*King for a Day*: five hundred drawings by McLean, each one inserted within a book listing the complete titles, exhibited at the Tate Gallery, London, as part of the exhibition 'Seven Artists'.

26. Peep toe piece (wearable).
27. Skliff, skluff clomp piece (wearable).
28. Run, jump, stand piece.
29. Sound piece for wearables, (shoes?).
30. Portrait of Barnes Pond by Alexander Saville work.
31. Taking it easy piece work/piece.
32. Disposable piece.
33. Throwaway piece.
34. Kickaway work.
35. Blowaway work.
36. Goodbye London piece.
37. Hallo New York, piece.
38. Round the world in half an hour piece. J. Saville.
39. Selection from the last day of the decade work piece.
40. Medley work from the last day of the Decade, wearables again.
41. Sculpture of the seasons.
42. Painting of the week, work.
43. Piece for Mecca Ballrooms (Moonrock shuffle).
44. My latest offering piece/thing.
45. 9 postcards of the Barnes Pond Area.
46. Torn tit book piece, (crimble crumble) found.
47. Painting piece (floor), portrait.
48. Wall painting piece, portrait.
49. Portrait for some people, work.
50. Song, joke and dance piece/thing/work.

# Oral Communication

I

My project will be to visit you in Paris, April, 1970, and there make clear the idea of oral communication as artform.

Ian Wilson exhibited in the seminal group exhibition, 'Information' (MOMA, New York, June 1970). His oral communication pieces were included in Lucy Lippard's anthology *Six Years: The Dematerialization of the Art Object from 1960 to 1972.* He is now rumoured to live in an ashram in New York State.

II
Ian Wilson came to Paris in January 1970 and talked about the idea of oral communication as artform.

Ian Wilson
**1970**

# Letter 4

Halla Beloff
Edinburgh
January 2002

Dear Reader,

The counter-culture was global – or so we thought. For the first time we felt in touch with California and Paris, Poland and India and together we could change the world. Even Edinburgh would move to a more open and humane and anarchic direction. It and we would be a tonic to the nation and the very idea of 'nation' would become irrelevant.

Scottish culture believed itself to be 'European' but surely it gloried in a powerful insularity too. And that was all to be moribund, this was a brave and new world and we had no irony in that belief. The dystopias of Huxley and Orwell were forgotten – we now had the key to happiness. And surprisingly even now, it still seems we were doing the right thing and it was good.

It was the New Art that was for me the most profound new way of thinking and the New Art was not unrelated to the new psychology and psychiatry. Those gates were opened by Richard Demarco and R. D. Laing, Ricky the more local influence and Laing the wider. Ricky to be pushed aside by financial strictures and the power of convention who took his ideas and made them their own, and Laing to be destroyed by his internal demons, which allowed the psychiatric establishment to sweep him away as a no-hoper.

The 'STRATEGY: GET ARTS' show all over Edinburgh College of Art was the 'event' of the Festival of 1970, although, as might be expected, not part of it. The opening was unforgettable – the mob, the champagne corks popping, the Fire Master in person insisting that the corridor of knives be covered by chicken wire there and then, Joseph Beuys present-ing himself as a work of art in the image of that man with the serious mien, the homburg hat, the boots and the fisherman's weskit. The whole Dusseldorf Art School caravan there to show us what conceptual art was and was to be. We didn't know then that we were seeing the birth of

Land Art, film loops instead of paintings, Sound Art with those endlessly banging doors and installations. The idea that an artist would present their identity as a 'work of art' was surely shown to us in those sleds carrying the neat rolls of felt and fat which represented the mythic saga of his rescue in the Russian steppe when his plane crashed in the War. That first venture has led directly to Tracy Emin's unmade bed, another index of identity, although few people have seen the connection. What we did know was that we were seeing a new iconoclasm and that we were having a terrific time. We were excited and we were never going to be the same again. From that day came the divide between painting as craft and art as a cognitive activity with wit and irony and enigma as the skill rather than the application of tonal values. The absence of the Art College staff at that critical 'happening' was a sign of the slow change that is the Edinburgh wont.

There were follow-ups, the most provocative being the '12 Hour Lecture' given by Beuys at the Melville College premises then in Melville Crescent where he did indeed 'lecture' but also drew on his famous blackboard and every now and again swept the floor. That sweeping was a provocative and symbolic gesture, which I think we did not decode at the time . . . Few stayed the course but again he was the Total Work of Art. Art as a form of revolutionary mysticism is still lurking on the continent, but here we have returned to the commercial dimension.

The Edinburgh Festival had a deserved reputation for bringing great productions and performances to us but if we felt that we were in touch with international ideas it was again through the work of Demarco. Kantor's theatre group provided a revolutionary experience and a new emotional dimension to sitting in the dark watching people tell you a story. They were accepted by the 'official' Festival to its great credit with *Wielepole Wielepole* presented at the Moray House Gymnasium.

Here we could see life in a Polish village not with the sentimentality of a Yiddish theatre or, heaven forfend, a fiddler on the roof, but with magic and realism and raw emotion that left some of us still weeping as we saw the old Lord Cameron bravely finding his way down those precarious bleachers. Again Kantor personally evoked an intellectual loyalty that outlasted his death. Such theatre ran counter not only to the old but to the rantings of the new John Osborne 'heroes'. This is about imagination transforming oppressive stormy experiences in the world of the War and showing us how soft we have been living here.

Ronnie Laing, whose *The Divided Self* (1960) was a brilliant humanistic approach to the pain of identity confusion, used to come to Edinburgh under the unlikely sponsorship of the University and other straight groups and give his meandering 'lectures' while clearly under the influence of a combination of drink and drugs. We were enlightened but also dreadfully embarrassed for him while he tried to maintain some thread among the long, long pauses. We never found it. My then twelve-year-old daughter says she was lastingly influenced by her experience of suffering with him as he tried to relate beautiful slides of the recently 'walked' moon with the philosophy of natural childbirth for a group of mid-wives and mothers. She couldn't imagine an intellectual so disconcerted.

All this while my young social worker friends were using the packed Assembly College Hall on a Sunday afternoon for a Transcendental Meditation meeting under the presence of the Maharishi himself, who gave the John Beloff short shrift when he tried in his usual way to contribute some reasonable concomitants of other consciousnesses. It was not all harmony.

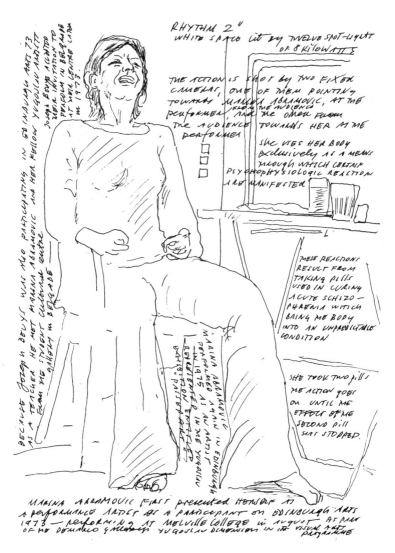

Richard Demarco
Marina Abramovic in performance
1974

## *from* Twenty Reflections and Resolutions of a Gallery Director on Facing the Art World of 1972

Gallery Directors have, above all, the responsibility to protect their artists from 'success' – in worldly terms.

∗

Where do you exhibit the art of those creative souls who prefer drawing with a ball thrown into the air, or footprints in wet sand, instead of with a brush or pencil on canvas or paper?

∗

All great artists reveal first their great LOVE of living. Their skills and even their virtuosity are relatively unimportant.

∗

Art Gallery Directors should take the vow of poverty, lest they be confused with dealers in antique furniture and 'objets d'art'.

∗

When will the Demarco gallery be invited to organise exhibitions in police stations, prisons, hospitals, in parks, on hilltops, in churches, at business conferences, as the focal points of political gatherings?

∗

The true artist is free of the turning of the calendar, and its division into days, months and years, so why, therefore, should the Gallery Director, who should also be principally a creator, be so confined?

How many Cabinet advisors or Lord Provosts or generals would take a Gallery Director seriously if they knew he was responsible for artists who rightly defined are constant threats in their roles as revolutionaries and prophets in a society they see as static and thus unnatural?

*

When I say an artwork is good or bad I am making not only an aesthetic judgement but, more importantly, a moral one.

*

If all the artists of Scotland had spoken with one voice in support of the Upper Clyde Shipworkers, would the U.C.S. problems have been solved?

*

I remember the prayer of St Francis Loyola for his Order of Jesuits, and pray that the Demarco Gallery will always be in travail and tested to the breaking point.

*

I regard the Demarco Gallery as a sculpture which is far from finished. Don't ask me how it is progressing. It is enough that I do it. I do not understand how it develops but I do know it does so only when I am prepared to scrap it and begin again and that is how I felt this New Year's Day, 1972.

Richard Demarco
**New Year's Day 1972**

Richard Demarco and Joseph Beuys
1970

First Year Design

Richard Demarco Gallery (1966–2002)
Edinburgh Arts Summer School(1972–1980)

STRATEGY: GET ARTS
Exhibition of new art, Edinburgh College of Art.
From left: Hete Hunnerman; Daniel Spoerri; Jennifer Gough-Cooper; unknown; unknown.
1970

Daniel Spoerri: 'The Banana-Trap Dinner'
(part of STRATEGY: GET ARTS)
From left: Ronald Mavor, Director SAC; unknown; Stanley Wright, Principal ECA;
Cordelia Oliver, Art Critic of the *Guardian*.
**1970**

## A Demarcation Line

A DEMARCATION LINE
must be made everywhere and always
quickly and firmly,
as it will function anyway
whatever we choose to do,
automatically
and relentlessly,
leaving us
at this side or the other.

if we make it
we shall have an impression
of a free choice
or an awareness of necessity,
even if we are the losers.

a demarcation line
emerges always and everywhere
it performs all possible roles
it assumes all possible forms
it is eternal
and immoral.
Backward
Presumptuous

settled
taking their seats
judges
jurors
opinion-makers
decision-makers
continuators
cultivating
their line
and their
individualities

ciquettes
pseudo-avant garde
propogating
thoughtlessly
and alarmingly
pseudo-avant garde
mass-producing
with consent
and unanimously

pseudo-avant garde
tamed
and legitimate
with testimonials
and credentials
battening on
myths
and all kinds of
sanctities
sinister
shamans
missionaries
prosperous
quack

the few

the unofficial

the neglected

refusing prestige

not afraid to
be ridiculous

the risk-taking

disinterested
but completely
without a chance
to be applied
or adjusted

without a chance
to give account
and justify

helpless

impossible

The exhibition
is no longer an indifferent means
of presenting and recording
    it becomes
an active environment

involving the audience in adventures and
traps,
refusing them and not satisfying
their reason of being
spectators
beholders
and visitors.

   The exhibition
does have a 'ready' reality, though;
it is my own creation and my own past
foreign and made objective
by getting mixed
with the matter of life.

Tadeusz Kantor
Part of "ATELIER '72", an exhibition of contemporary Polish artists,
The Richard Demarco Gallery, Edinburgh International Festival,
1972

Tadeusz Kantor
*Lovelies and Dowdies* at Poorhouse Theatre (Sean Connery in audience)
**1973**

Demarco Gallery (2) v Scottish Arts Council (4)
Inverleith Park, Edinburgh
**1973**

Joseph Beuys visits Scotland
1974

'On the trip to Edinburgh, I had absolutely no idea of what I was going to do. Upon my arrival, I saw an old staff. It seemed to be important; I needed it … The place was important. I say we only live once on this planet as a living organism, so the place in which we live plays an important role. Initially as a simple question: What is Scotland? What is it? … I put out my antennae and immediately received impressions. Immediately. Impressions that I had been carrying around inside of me for a long time: Scotland, King Arthur's Round Table, the story of the Holy Grail. These elements combined and continued to work in me …' (JB)

From interview with Beuys by Hagen Lieberknecht

Edinburgh Arts, Royal Botanical Gardens
From left: Joseph Beuys, Lady Roseberry, Buckminster Fuller.
**1974**

Buckminster Fuller lecturing at Black & White Oil Conference, Edinburgh Arts.
**1974**

Jimmy Boyle released from Barlinnie Prison Special Unit to meet Joseph Beuys
From left: Phil Hitchcock and Jane Whitaker (Edinburgh Arts participants);
Jimmy Boyle; Special Unit Prison Officers.
**1974**

cricot
Kantor
cricot
Kantor
LOVELIES AND DOWDIES
LOVELIES AND DOWDIES
HILL
Kantor
cricot
Kantor

Edinburgh Arts Summer School
David Helder signals to students on Salisbury Crags below.
**1972**

Edinburgh Arts participants directed by David Helder from Arthur's Seat
1972

'Edinburgh Arts' tentatives towards a reintegration of the arts and social consciousness are much needed. The plea for discovery rather than progress, for focus upon pre-Renaissance pasts, for the establishment of new roots for art, will hopefully contribute to a clearer look at the motives for making art at this time, as well as to that network which is necessary to the survival, or revival, of a meaningful and communicable art.' (Lucy Lippard)

Edinburgh Arts Summer School
Temple Wood Stone Circle, Kilmartin Glen, Argyll.
**1976**

Tom McGrath recently asked me to do an article on 'Culture'. At first I said "No, I couldn't do that – I don't know enough about it". I imagined myself toiling away down in the Mitchell Library, reading up everything I could find on the 'subject', before I dared open my mouth. Then I realised that this hesitancy on my part was caused by that very aspect of how culture *works* in this society that I in fact feel quite strongly about. So stuff going down to the Mitchell.

Here's a university past-paper question on English Literature – it's one taken literally at random from some I've been looking at recently: ' "Their imagery is rarely decorative, it is used to intensify their meaning. And it is through their imagery that we can distinguish their very different concepts of the relationship of man to God." Discuss with reference to two or more of the Metaphysical poets.' Well, discuss but not in a Glasgow accent: simulate the middle class modulations and *bon-mots* of the question to 'discuss', in an exam hall with your brain packed with 'key quotes' on your way to £2,000 a year, the different ideas some men had on 'the relationship of man to God'. Is nothing sacred? No, nothing is as far as the university is concerned; and the university is at the heart of the perpetuation of the 'culture' myth. The university (and here I speak specifically about the Arts faculties) is a reification of the notion that culture is synonymous with property. And the essentially acquisitive attitude to culture, 'education', and 'a good accent' is simply an aspect of the competitive, status-conscious class structure of the society as a whole ... where beauty in language is recognised as the property of a particular class, then naturally truth is assumed to be the property of that class also. So a person who doesn't 'speak right' is therefore categorised as an ignoramus; it's not simply that he doesn't know how to speak right, but that this 'inability' shows that he has no claim to knowledge of truth. That supposed insult 'the language of the gutter' puts forward a revealing metaphor for society. The working-class rubbish, with all its bad pronunciation and dreadful swearwords, is only really fit for draining away out of sight ... It's the system that ensures that 'culture', like everything else, is blasphemed into something to do with ownership, something to do with defining oneself – according to one's cultural tastes – on the hierarchy of power and status ... Where 'culture' is something to do with 'leisure', and 'leisure' is the opposite of 'work', then trying to improve in whatever way, or make more accessible, works of culture, is simply trying to make more pleasant, or relevant, the various compensations of leisure that are usually gathered under the one label 'the standard of living'. But it's a mode of living that people should be striving for, not just a 'standard'. The trouble is that when one recognises this, one also recognises that a satisfactory mode of being is only fully possible when work and leisure are synonymous. Not synonymous in the sense of being absolutely identical, but at least not being, as they are now, diametrically opposed to each other, where for the most people the latter is a form of compensation for the former ... But I've gone on long enough, and I don't see the point of trying to make a synthesis ... I'm on £4 per thousand words for this article, which is really quite generous – but the length of time I've spent thinking about it, it's actually working out about four bob an hour, which means that in an hour's work on this, I'll have earned the same amount as a cleaner earns in washing three university corridors: or putting it another way, I'll have earned as much in one hour as the future Professor Emeritus of Working-Class Culture will earn in the time it takes him to leave one muddy footprint.

Tom Leonard
First published in *Scottish International*
**1973**

25th January 1973

Dear Stephen Willats,

I was most interested to read about your exhibition in the *Studio International*. I feel your researches are both imaginative and relevant in the community today. At Edinburgh College of Art we are organising an events week on the theme 'The artist and the community' and I am very keen that you should come up to Scotland for the day and explain and perhaps exhibit your ideas on the question.

Our college is an institution which is dominated by a practical approach to Art Education. Whether or not this is the best way of organising courses it should not, in my opinion, be done at the exclusion of the conceptual aspects of Art. Many of the students who leave the college, although they are good practitioners, find they are unable to relate what they are doing to the community at large.

I am anxious not to miss the opportunity of including your work in the exhibitions and discussions that will be taking place. I enclose a rather official form which I hope you will be able to fill in.

If you are able to come to Edinburgh I will of course be only too happy to pay all the expenses you require. The basic expenses will be your travelling expenses costs plus a normal lecturing fee for the day £15. The dates for the events which have not been quite finalised are the 26th, 27th and 28th of March.

I hope you can come.

Yours sincerely,

Angus MacLean
President Students Representative Council

Stephen Willats
London
January 2002

### The Edinburgh Social Model Construction Project

The invitation to the 'Three Day Event' taking place at Edinburgh College of Art came out of the blue, but immediately I felt here was an opportunity, rare at the time, to present my ideas in a context that was going to be receptive. In Edinburgh I was given the opportunity to discuss my work seriously, in a context of some rebellion, for it was the students of the College who had set up the event in rejection of what they felt were outmoded teaching practices.

The first visit to Edinburgh became the starting point for an association with the city that lasted several years, in which I got to know its streets and bars pretty well, and especially became acquainted with the night-train between Kings Cross and Waverley. The reaction to my presentation at the 'Three Day Event' was extremely enthusiastic and the idea that something actual should follow seemed a necessary and logical outcome. The possibility quickly arose when, again out of the blue, I received a letter from John Mason who was organising a Festival in Leith to coincide, maybe even compete, with the 1973 Edinburgh Festival. Having met John, I realised I had the opportunity to develop what was to be the most complete and radical expression of my work to date. The work was conceived as a sequence of feedback loops between four communities and a central Core, the requirement for deciding on the four communities being that they were geographically, socially, and economically separated.

I started work in Edinburgh rather as though I were working in Paris or Berlin: I assumed that I was going to work in another country, that I was on an act of personal discovery. This was an important initial decision because I realised that I needed to work with people who had an intimate knowledge of Edinburgh, who could develop the work and act as an interface, so I would be in a kind of co-operation with them.

Fortunately the students, now ex-students, from the Art School were very willing to get involved at this level (in particular John Wilde). This group of volunteers was formalised in the conceptual model of the work as 'Project Operators', a small group that looked after all aspects of the work in a defined area of streets called a 'Project Area'. From a few days' reconnaissance, driving around every conceivable district of Edinburgh in an old battered Morris Minor, four areas were selected – Project Area One: Leith; Project Area Two: Morningside; Project Area Three: Slateford; Project Area Four: Silverknowes.

The feedback loop was actualised by a set of procedures carried out by Project Operators in a twenty-four-hour cycle, over five days. Each day focussed all four communities' attention on a Problem Area that concerned people's daily lives. An important aim of the work was to externalise, for both individuals and communities, the inherent relativity of social perception and belief. To show that nothing has to be fixed, that reality is fluid and transient and can be transformed to represent different priorities and attitudes, the transformation from one thing into another being a creative act.

In order to facilitate people's participation in the work a lot of hard footwork had to be done; the process of contextualisation had to be started. I set about loading it with visual references, and creating areas of attention for the work that would already be meaningful to residents. Shops, a golf club, and at Leith the Community Centre became sites for Public Register Boards on which were to be displayed Problem Sheets completed by participants in the work. Problem Sheets were the main agent in the feedback process between Central Core and participants and contained questions, diagrams and photographs that invited individuals to make a writing, drawing or diagram in response.

A routine was established, and each day a new set of three Problem Sheets was delivered to participants in the morning, then in the afternoon they were collected and taken to the Central Core, situated in an office in the ICL computing centre at Dalkeith. The function of the feedback loop between Central Core and the participants was that the new questions could be created from the consensus tendencies expressed in the previous cycle, the idea being that over the five days the work would come to reflect areas of agreement between the people involved. Consequently it was desirable that problem situations should not be known in advance. Rank Xerox had just opened a copy shop in George Street importing this new technology to Scotland for the first time. Without much persuasion they agreed to act as our sponsor as a means of demonstrating the potential of Xeroxing. The implications of instant free copying were enormous: new Problem Sheets could be created first thing in the morning, and then distributed to participants by 10 am. Stuart Pound, a renowned computer programmer, negotiated with ICL at Dalkeith for us to have access each evening to their main frame computers, so that we could run a program devised to examine completed forms and assess consensus tendencies for each Project Area. The resulting statements of 'consensus' for each Project Area then formed the basis for new questions selected in the program from a store of possible problem combinations. These were rewritten or recomposed as necessary to amplify the direction of the priorities expressed.

The contemporary language for computers was called FORTRAN and was simply not up to the job. As the evening of our first attempt to process Problem Sheets wore on it became apparent the project would fail if we continued with FORTRAN. Quick improvisation was required. A Central Core committee was formed (and met in a room at the Edinburgh Regional Computing Centre, Allison House in Nicholson

Square) to enact the computer program by hand – the process being undertaken by twelve people sitting around a large table. What was envisaged as taking half an hour or so now took all night. The one abiding memory I have of being in Edinburgh is sitting in an anonymous somewhat dark room shifting through and arguing over Problem Sheets as the night got colder and colder, made easier by a swig of Bells substandard whisky mixed with lemonade to make it drinkable – obtained cheap from a man at the railway sidings. Having eventually reached agreement, arrived at consensus tendencies statement devised the new problems and typed them up on master Problem Sheets, it was quickly up and off to Rank Xerox for 8.30 am. It worked and the project was able to continue.

The real success of the project was made by the Project Operators, for at this level the work was all about one-to-one human relationships – going from door to door and introducing the idea of participation to whoever answered. Project Operators for a particular area thus got to know everyone, and as they had to call twice a day, giving out new Problem Sheets in the morning and collecting completed ones around teatime, they soon got quite involved with people, stepping inside for endless cups of tea, and in one case an evening meal.

The Project Operators in each area also maintained the Public Register Boards, attaching to them completed Problem Sheets once they had been processed by the Central Core, and often throughout the day a Project Operator was also in attendance to talk with visitors. Anyone could visit the Public Register Boards. Neighbourhood leaflets about them were distributed, but the most powerful pull of curiosity was generated by word of mouth. The Public Register Boards immediately became an 'event' in the neighbourhoods, something that should be seen regardless of whether you were a participant, and they acted as a focal point, a meeting between residents, who often stayed around them quite a while, particularly at Silverknowes Golf Club.

As the work progressed through the daily cycle of events it certainly generated more and more interest in the neighbourhoods, to the point where after five exhausting days people told us they didn't want the work to stop. The open display of participants' responses (without comment) was to stimulate people to make their responses over the five days, how they had started to embody other people's ideas, and opinions from their own Project Area and importantly also from others.

The invitation from John Mason also provided me personally with a very direct contact with people, and provided experiences that would be hard to obtain normally. Particularly interesting to me was the Project Area at Morningside, which, while well known in Edinburgh, was to me wholly unknown. I worked in the Morningside area, and while going from door to door inviting participation, I came to the house of two very elderly sisters who were senior members of the Scottish Academy. I explained my ideas on the doorstep to one of the sisters, and before I could finish a bony hand came out and pulled me inside. It was dark and gloomy, but it slowly became apparent that there were few furnishings or comforts, just wall-to-wall stacks of paintings in heavy wooden frames, hundreds of Scottish landscapes. As I sat on a stool in the middle of the room with the two sisters on each side – a naked light bulb dangling just above me – they pulled out two long metal ear trumpets and, aiming them in my direction, proceeded to quiz me about the project. In fact the sister on the doorstep had not heard a thing I had said, so now I bellowed my explanations into the middle space between the two ear trumpets. They were both very alert, eager to know more, and with their shrill Morningside accents got more and more animated. One made me a mug of tea so I had to stay longer, in fact over an hour. They were very enthusiastic about what were to them wholly new ideas about 'art', its social function, the role of the audience, etc., and not only did they agree to participate, but did so right through the work. I often wonder who they actually were, as it was policy not to ask for names.

The Social Resource Project took place at the same time as the Edinburgh Festival, and we managed to get included as a listing on the Fringe handouts. But that is all the official response we got, and I remember feeling at the time how incredible it was that here was a radical artwork involving so many people from Edinburgh, that was an expression of their lives, their perceptions of the environment, etc., and yet it was being totally ignored by the press, critics and the Festival audience. This despite the high neighbourhood profile the work achieved with posters, explanatory handout leaflets and information we sent to all local and national press.

Stephen Willats

Willats presented a paper about *The Edinburgh Social Model Construction Project* at the Computer Art Society Symposium that formed part of the Official Fringe in 1973. A more detailed description of the project is given in *Art and Social Function*, Willats, 1976 republished by Ellipsis, London, 2001. Also in 'The Edinburgh Project', *Art and Artists*, January 1974. vol 8., No. 10, which gives a contemporary account. An archive about the work is in the collection of the SNGMA.

# SOCIAL MODEL CONSTRUCTION PROJECT

**PROJECT DATES, AUGUST 25th – 31st.**

THE SOCIAL MODEL CONSTRUCTION PROJECT IS AN ART WORK THAT ENABLES PEOPLE RESIDENT IN FOUR AREAS OF EDINBURGH TO ARTICULATE THE WAY THEY PERCEIVE AND UNDERSTAND CONVENTIONS THAT DETERMINE PEOPLES RELATIONSHIPS TO EACH OTHER. PARTICIPANTS IN THE PROJECT ARE GIVEN A SERIES OF TASKS WHICH CONSIST OF DEVISING AND RECORDING SOLUTIONS TO PROBLEMS CONCERNED WITH HOW THEY SEE PERSON TO PERSON INTER-ACTION. THE SOLUTIONS TO THE PROBLEMS ARE FED INTO A COMPUTING SYSTEM THAT FORMULATES NEW PROBLEMS FROM THEM, AND THESE ARE THEN GIVEN TO PARTICIPANTS. THIS LOOP PROCESS OCCURS EACH DAY FOR FIVE DAYS. AS THE BASIS OF THE PROBLEMS USED IN THE PROJECT IS DETERMINED BY THE SOLUTIONS TO PROCEDING ONES IT IS ENVISAGED THAT A LEARNING PROCESS WILL EVOLVE IN A SELF-DETERMINED HIERACHY OF INFORMATION, THE CONTENTS OF WHICH GRADUALLY BECOME MORE MEANINGFUL AND RELEVANT TO PARTICIPANTS AS IT PROGRESSES. PUBLIC MONITORS HAVE BEEN SET UP TO DISPLAY PARTICIPANTS SOLUTIONS TO THE PROBLEMS THEY HAVE BEEN GIVEN. THE NEAREST PUBLIC MONITOR TO THIS PROJECT AREA IS AT.

## PROJECT AREA ONE

COCHRANE PLACE.       FINGZIES PLACE.
PARKVALE PLACE.       ELM PLACE.
ROSEVALE PLACE.       NOBLE PLACE.
SUMMERFIELD PLACE.    LINDEAN PLACE.

PROJECT ADDRESS, 19, STEWART TERRACE, EDINBURGH.

# SOCIAL MODEL CONSTRUCTION PROJECT

**PROJECT DATES, AUGUST 25th – 31st.**

THE SOCIAL MODEL CONSTRUCTION PROJECT IS AN ART WORK THAT ENABLES PEOPLE RESIDENT IN FOUR AREAS OF EDINBURGH TO ARTICULATE THE WAY THEY PERCEIVE AND UNDERSTAND CONVENTIONS THAT DETERMINE PEOPLES RELATIONSHIPS TO EACH OTHER. PARTICIPANTS IN THE PROJECT ARE GIVEN A SERIES OF TASKS WHICH CONSIST OF DEVISING AND RECORDING SOLUTIONS TO PROBLEMS CONCERNED WITH HOW THEY SEE PERSON TO PERSON INTER-ACTION. THE SOLUTIONS TO THE PROBLEMS ARE FED INTO A COMPUTING SYSTEM THAT FORMULATES NEW PROBLEMS FROM THEM, AND THESE ARE THEN GIVEN TO PARTICIPANTS. THIS LOOP PROCESS OCCURS EACH DAY FOR FIVE DAYS. AS THE BASIS OF THE PROBLEMS USED IN THE PROJECT IS DETERMINED BY THE SOLUTIONS TO PROCEDING ONES IT IS ENVISAGED THAT A LEARNING PROCESS WILL EVOLVE IN A SELF-DETERMINED HIERACHY OF INFORMATION, THE CONTENTS OF WHICH GRADUALLY BECOME MORE MEANINGFUL AND RELEVANT TO PARTICIPANTS AS IT PROGRESSES. PUBLIC MONITORS HAVE BEEN SET UP TO DISPLAY PARTICIPANTS SOLUTIONS TO THE PROBLEMS THEY HAVE BEEN GIVEN. THE NEAREST PUBLIC MONITOR TO THIS PROJECT AREA IS AT.

## PROJECT AREA FOUR

SILVERKNOWES ROAD.    SILVERKNOWES PLACE.
SILVERKNOWES GDNS.    SILVERKNOWES COURT.
SILVERKNOWES GROVE.   SILVERKNOWES BANK.
          SILVERKNOWES EASTWAY.

PROJECT ADDRESS, 19 STEWART TERRACE, EDINBUGH.

# SOCIAL MODEL CONSTRUCTION PROJECT

**PROJECT DATES, AUGUST 25th – 31st.**

THE SOCIAL MODEL CONSTRUCTION PROJECT IS AN ART WORK THAT ENABLES PEOPLE RESIDENT IN FOUR AREAS OF EDINBURGH TO ARTICULATE THE WAY THEY PERCEIVE AND UNDERSTAND CONVENTIONS THAT DETERMINE PEOPLES RELATIONSHIPS TO EACH OTHER. PARTICIPANTS IN THE PROJECT ARE GIVEN A SERIES OF TASKS WHICH CONSIST OF DEVISING AND RECORDING SOLUTIONS TO PROBLEMS CONCERNED WITH HOW THEY SEE PERSON TO PERSON INTER-ACTION. THE SOLUTIONS TO THE PROBLEMS ARE FED INTO A COMPUTING SYSTEM THAT FORMULATES NEW PROBLEMS FROM THEM, AND THESE ARE THEN GIVEN TO PARTICIPANTS. THIS LOOP PROCESS OCCURS EACH DAY FOR FIVE DAYS. AS THE BASIS OF THE PROBLEMS USED IN THE PROJECT IS DETERMINED BY THE SOLUTIONS TO PROCEDING ONES IT IS ENVISAGED THAT A LEARNING PROCESS WILL EVOLVE IN A SELF-DETERMINED HIERACHY OF INFORMATION, THE CONTENTS OF WHICH GRADUALLY BECOME MORE MEANINGFUL AND RELEVANT TO PARTICIPANTS AS IT PROGRESSES. PUBLIC MONITORS HAVE BEEN SET UP TO DISPLAY PARTICIPANTS SOLUTIONS TO THE PROBLEMS THEY HAVE BEEN GIVEN. THE NEAREST PUBLIC MONITOR TO THIS PROJECT AREA IS AT.

## PROJECT AREA THREE

WARDLAW STREET.       WARDLAW PLACE.
WARDLAW TERRACE.      STEWART TERRACE.
WHEATFIELD STREET.    SMITHFIELD STREET.

PROJECT ADDRESS, 19 STEWART TERRACE, EDINBURGH.

# SOCIAL MODEL CONSTRUCTION PROJECT

**PROJECT DATES, AUGUST 25th – 31st.**

THE SOCIAL MODEL CONSTRUCTION PROJECT IS AN ART WORK THAT ENABLES PEOPLE RESIDENT IN FOUR AREAS OF EDINBURGH TO ARTICULATE THE WAY THEY PERCEIVE AND UNDERSTAND CONVENTIONS THAT DETERMINE PEOPLES RELATIONSHIPS TO EACH OTHER. PARTICIPANTS IN THE PROJECT ARE GIVEN A SERIES OF TASKS WHICH CONSIST OF DEVISING AND RECORDING SOLUTIONS TO PROBLEMS CONCERNED WITH HOW THEY SEE PERSON TO PERSON INTER-ACTION. THE SOLUTIONS TO THE PROBLEMS ARE FED INTO A COMPUTING SYSTEM THAT FORMULATES NEW PROBLEMS FROM THEM, AND THESE ARE THEN GIVEN TO PARTICIPANTS. THIS LOOP PROCESS OCCURS EACH DAY FOR FIVE DAYS. AS THE BASIS OF THE PROBLEMS USED IN THE PROJECT IS DETERMINED BY THE SOLUTIONS TO PROCEDING ONES IT IS ENVISAGED THAT A LEARNING PROCESS WILL EVOLVE IN A SELF-DETERMINED HIERACHY OF INFORMATION, THE CONTENTS OF WHICH GRADUALLY BECOME MORE MEANINGFUL AND RELEVANT TO PARTICIPANTS AS IT PROGRESSES. PUBLIC MONITORS HAVE BEEN SET UP TO DISPLAY PARTICIPANTS SOLUTIONS TO THE PROBLEMS THEY HAVE BEEN GIVEN. THE NEAREST PUBLIC MONITOR TO THIS PROJECT AREA IS AT.

## PROJECT AREA TWO

WOODBURN TERRACE.     BRAID AVENUE.
NILE GROVE.           CLUNY AVENUE.
CLUNY TERRACE.        CLUNY PLACE.

PROJECT ADDRESS, 19 STEWART TERRACE, EDINBURGH.

# The Incidental Person

I have a new impression of London-based Britain from Edinburgh. What seems to be difficult in London, for many diverse reasons, the Scottish Office appears to be more ready to consider. APG [Artists Placement Group] has worked-out with this Department a form of association the feasibility of which is now being studied, and it is a long way from the connotations of the term 'artist in residence' ...

Perhaps we should dispense with the public use of this word artist, in the same way that we are supposed to be dispensing with sex-discriminatory and value-judging language. APG has put forward alternatives from time to time, Incidental Person having some advantages, if referring to one in whom certain specially formulative capabilities show up. There is a tendency for society to abandon such a person, who then comes under impossible pressures ...

Ground-level 'politics' are a form of sectional-interest civil war. Even if you take politics to mean the ideological see-saw, an Incidental Person on the site takes the stand of a third ideological position which is off the plane of their obvious collision-areas. The function is more to watch the doings and listen to the noises, and to eliminate from output the signs of a received idea as being of the work. In doing this, (s)he represents people who would not accept their premises, time-bases, ambitions, formulations, as valid, and who will occupy the scene later. Our present conventional assumptions are making for confusion in the long term unless an undertaking succeeds in gearing itself to a long-term, real process. 'Knowledge' is a modern equivalent for the opium once said to be religion ...

My personal view of causes include the mental furniture industry and the Arts Council – they have arranged matters to ensure that no radically new idea comes to the fore if they can possibly avoid it ... We have become not humans but a species of rodent.

John Latham from *Studio International*
March–April, 1976

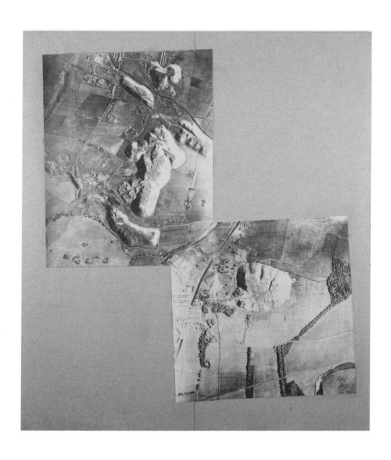

The Artists Placement Group and the Scottish Office nominated three areas for attention in this period of association – Urban Renewal, Derelict Land, and Graphics.
Above: John Latham, 'Niddrie Woman'.

1977

where
there
going
are
you
where
Watch

THE PATH

David Harding and Alan Bold, 'Poetry Path' (Glenrothes).
Constructed upon 'Desire Lines' – pathways made by residents rather
than designated by planners. David Harding was Town Artist
at Glenrothes 1968–1978, and went on to help establish the
Environmental Art Course at Glasgow School of Art in 1986.
**1977**

REGULAR PRESENTS
THE
BACK FROM TAKING LONDON!
AT TIFFANY'
PLUS VERANDAH
— LATE BAR! -

ARE EVEN MORE ALRIGHT!
ON TUES. 2ND MAY
OYS - 75P
AT DOOR
REGULAR MUSIC
DIO
RTH
J.
Mike Gower!

# Letter 6

Malcolm Dickson
Glasgow
February 2002

Dear Reader,

It's my fortieth birthday next week, so I've been looking back in many ways with the excuse of seeing ahead more clearly. I have been pulling on threads that lead me to the spare room which is packed with detritus – bin bags full of baby clothes, electrical appliances, books. In here, there is an archive of sorts. Several boxes of video tapes contain documentation of the Chomsky conference (as it's come to be known) at the Pearce Institute in Govan; The Next Five Minutes festival of media activism at the Paradiso in Amsterdam, bits and bobs from the Radical Black and Third World Bookfair in Partick Borough Halls; and readings by Jim Kelman, Tom Leonard and Jeff Torrington at Transmission in 1986. These events were landmarks in my education. I find audio tapes from Free University talks – Jo Spence, Roland Miller, Stefan Szczelkun – and the launch of 'Workers City' at Hatchards (5 August 1988); Super-8 film footage from 'The Burning' in Glasgow Green on (8 August 1988). Anxiety creeps in – all this stuff just scrapes the surface of things ... But then, there is something meaningful in hoarding. I will get it all digitised, that might mean that some of it may be repurposed some day soon.

*

1980–84. There was a resurgence of anarchist ideas and the Glasgow group held meetings which were often packed with people. Glasgow Bookshop Collective was the centre of a spider's web for alternative culture. We kind of tried to set up a pirate radio station but had too many meetings about it rather than doing it. The guy with the transmitter, and therefore the power, suggested in a seriously supportive kind of way that me and Peter Thomson go for elocution lessons. Luckily his flat was burgled and transmitter nicked. Property, after all, is theft.

*Variant* 1987. Relaunched with Issue 3 and a party in Alasdair Gray's house. I don't remember much. There were three magazines that were all part of a broadening of culture for me at that time – *Variant*, *Here & Now* and *Edinburgh Review*. *Variant* gave expression to a range of non-mainstream views on the arts, culture and politics – it included dissenting views and supported a diversity of creativity. Like the culture and scene it was a part of, it was non-parochial, while still very much rooted in the place from where it emanated. It also tried to make links laterally across media. Issue 6 gave away a badge which asked its wearers to 'Burn all illusions'. On the cover was a photograph from the solarised video of 'The Burning'.

1988–89. The Data Attic, Dundee. 'The Burning' was part of the Festival of Non-Participation, a decentralised event in Scotland. Playful, and serious, it was organised mainly by Pete Horobin. I lived in his flat (aka The DATA archive) in Union Street, Dundee for a year. Pete was a link to a whole new network of alternative art. In 1990 he changed his name to Marshall Anderson and continued to contribute to *Variant* with some fine investigative pieces of writing. The last time I met him was at a seminar on interventionist performance at Street Level as part of an event organised by Ross Birrell. With the millennium, he changed his identity again and moved to Ireland, allegedly. There's a show to be made of that decade and if you read this Pete, get in touch, wherever and whoever you are.

1989 Glasgow Cross. I'm in Clydeside Press folding and stapling copies of *Variant 7*. The front cover contained the statement 'History is made by those who say no.' That issue also contained multiple stickers by Mark Pawson, prints by Gordon Muir and Euan Sutherland. An audio cassette was produced, compiled by Billy Clark, with music, audio artworks, and noise. Two versions of a video magazine were available at the time – one dealing with video art, the other linking culture and politics in interviews with Hamish Henderson, John Taylor Caldwell, Farquhar McLay and James D. Young. Tommy, the printer, introduced me to Robert King who was assembling the pages for his magazine *Total*. As well as a print version, it included a CD of music – I still play it, but only when in the right mood. I've known him for fifteen years now but only last week did we discover that a mutual inspiration to do things was Scritti Politti's 'Skanc Bloc Bologna' – a 45 which had a breakdown of exactly how little it costs to do a record on its crudely printed cover.

1987–91. The Free University was 'established' in recognition of the potential in cultural activity to push things along and make connections between people. It was about breaking down isolation and people linking up with one another. Listening to a tape from a discussion held in October 1987, a mapping is discussed – 'cross recognition', kindred spirits, shaking people out of the impossibility of action, behave as if you had power and act as you mean to go on, a complete intolerance of rigid specialisms. It was also concerned with different ways that people could get together in a place that didn't shut at 5 pm and which didn't require you to spend money to be there. As well as the core groups meeting to discuss a space, fortnightly meetings were held on subjects as diverse as football, pop music, sexual politics (I cringe at the thought of one where an Andrea Dworkin text was read out and the men then had to leave the room to discuss it, then return, and the two groups compared notes. What a slagging!), Joseph Beuys, Paulo Freire, the German Green Movement, computers in the workplace, art and class. Two larger public meetings took place which focussed on the need to be more active in the public realm – the Culture & Politics seminar (July 1987); the Scratch Parliament (1988). Such liberatory ideas were echoed in the *Edinburgh Review* under the editorship of Peter Kravitz.

January 1990. The culmination of the eighties was Self-Determination & Power. Bringing together writers, artists, community workers, anarchists, socialists, nationalists (a few), Christians (fewer), tenants-group representatives, anti-racist campaigners, publishers, women's aid workers, teachers, such a phenomenal mix of people from different backgrounds. A banner decorates the platform behind the speakers emblazoned with the names of groups and magazines involved – Free University, *Scottish Child*, *Edinburgh Review*, *Here & Now*, *Variant*, *West Coast Magazine*, *Common Sense*, Clydeside Press, Scotia Bar.

Whilst dealing with the present and the future, the event provides a link between a Scottish tradition of enlightenment thought and Common Sense philosophy which says that everyone can know and everyone has the right to freedom. The keynote speakers were Noam Chomsky and George Davie. An aim, as it was with the Free University, was to stress the need for non-institutional support groups to be in touch with one another through informal networks.

The eighties were about making something that was unformed and invisible, tangible and real. It was smaller and it was easier to get in touch with others and to make an impact – in most cases the producers of the culture were also its audience. You have to look back to see forward, and the links continue to be made. Lineages can be teased out but history cannot be written because it never stops developing.

Malcolm Dickson

# The Only Conditions

The West has been ferocious barbaric imperative and consuming
I love the West
It has ransacked the world
It has destroyed simple people everywhere
It has emptied the world of meaning
Its wars have made nonsense of its religion
It has brought the world to the edge of destruction
It is blind one-sided materialist death-dealing ignorant and vicious
And I love it
Because it is acting as the other hand of God:
It is closing every door but *the* door
It has mocked every truth but *the* truth
It is bringing the world to its knees
It is bringing humanity into degradation despair and suffering
The only conditions out of which sleeping people
Can learn
To become

Alan Jackson
**1979**

# ma language is disgraceful

right inuff
ma language is disgraceful

ma maw tellt mi
ma teacher tellt mi
thi doactir tellt mi
thi priest tellt mi

ma boss tellt mi
ma landlady in carrington street tellt mi
thi lassie ah tried tay get aff way in 1969 tellt mi
sum wee smout thit thoat ah hudny read chomsky tellt mi
a calvinistic communist thit thoat ah wuz revisionist tellt mi

po-faced literati grimly kerryin thi burden a thi past tellt mi
po-faced literati grimly kerryin thi burden a thi future tellt mi
ma wife tellt mi jist-tay-git-inty-this-poem tellt mi
ma wainz came hame fray school an tellt mi
jist aboot ivry book ah oapnd tellt mi
even thi introduction tay thi Scottish National Dictionary tellt mi

ach well
all livin language is sacred
fuck thi lohta thim

Tom Leonard
from *Ghostie Men*
**1980**

*from* Situations Theoretical and Contemporary

We have decided to make Scotland secure.
This is strategically essential.
No question.

Scottish people have nothing to fear.
Noise pollution should not be a problem.
And all construction work will be landscaped.

We have decided to make America secure.
This is strategically essential.
No question.

Scottish people have nothing to fear.
Noise pollution should not be a problem.
And all construction work will be landscaped.

Today is National Income Card-Carrying Day.
On this day all citizens must wear cards prominently declaring their total income from all sources for the previous twelve months.

How full the underground shelters are this morning.
All those advocates of 'tighter control of the money supply'.
And there is that expert on 'international terrorism'.
Quite a card, eh?

Quick though – there goes the Chancellor of the Exchequer.
Oh dear. No pep-talk today!

And their judges spoke with one dialect,
but the condemned spoke with many voices.

And the prisons were full of many voices,
but never the dialect of the judges.

And the judges said:
                    "No-one is above the Law."

Scotland has become an independent socialist republic.
At last.

Eh?
You pinch yourself.
Jesus Christ. You've slept in again.

Tom Leonard
**1985**

Dear Reader,

To make this short appraisal of Pete Horobin and the DATA project it is important to understand the circumstances of his artistic background. Studying at Duncan of Jordanstone College of Art (DoJ) in the early 1970s he was constantly at loggerheads with the establishment. His anti-authority stance eventually led to DATA, but at the time Horobin found himself in a School of Drawing and Painting that was dated and unsympathetic to his interest in photography and his intuitive experiments with found materials and assemblage.

Kurt Schwitters died the year before he was born, yet for Horobin his art was still vital and alive. Joseph Beuys had been to Edinburgh, but a Ricky Demarco rant did little more than confuse and disturb students in a department where discourse with the staff was restricted to painting. A copy of Lucy Lippard's *Six Years: The Dematerialization of the Art Object*, which had miraculously survived in the college library, became Horobin's bible.

Moving further away from his Dundee peers philosophically and blissfully ignorant of key movements in contemporary art, Horobin faced towards Europe for guidance. He acknowledges the single most significant influence on him was a telepathic experience that occurred in 1977 while lying on a beach in St Tropez, when he experienced a sudden awakening to art's true potential (attributed to the proximity of Ben Vautier, living nearby in Nice). Later that year Horobin produced his first manifesto, *The Accessibility of the Art Object*, and then in 1978, in harmony with punk and the zeitgeist, he mailed original collages to randomly selected recipients, attracting the attention of the Special Branch in Dundee.

Horobin had crossed his rubicon and, on 01.01.80, embarked on DATA (Daily Action Time Archive, or Dix Ans Travaille Archive), a ten-year self-historification project. From its commencement his intention was to document the life of an ordinary artist whose origins lay in a non-artistic, working-class family. The rigorous process of documentation became far more than this, and the resulting archive containing original artworks, collaborations and the ephemera of daily life, is a fascinating insight into the 1980s.

DATA had its roots in conceptualism. It was a serious attempt to propose 'data' as an alternative to 'art' – his use of the word also anticipating the electronic digital age. In the interests of this book, it would be true to say that Horobin did not consider what he was doing as 'counterculture': at this point he was too ignorant of what culture actually was to think of attacking it. His quest was to discover and participate in contemporary culture – he believed the role of the artist was to work with the media of his time, and the media of his time was not paint.

Aware of his own virility and mortality, Horobin wished to record this fecund and energetic period of his life. The quintessential daily action that formed the basis of DATA was stenciling the date, a fundamental declaration: *I am alive.* Further daily actions were documented, photocopied and collated into a monthly loose-leaf magazine, posted to a mix of people in Scotland and abroad. Within months direct exchanges had been established with such artists as Peter Below (Germany) and Robin Crozier (England), who played significant roles in the development of DATA. Horobin had entered mail art, the vital free-flowing energy, Robert Filliou's 'Eternal Network'.

The project was also a statement of what was possible at a given time with limited resources. DATA was not exhibited in conventional galleries, as Horobin had no desire to re-enter the self-conscious world of galleries, selection committees and middle-class collectors. Mail art projects were completely democratic – anyone could be an artist.

Horobin was perversely and paradoxically isolationist – as far as he was concerned Scottish artists were completely out of touch with the type of activities DATA engaged in. In June 1982 he responded to an invitation from Peter Below, and hitch-hiked to The Neoist Network's 'First European Training Camp' in Wurzburg (Germany). Expecting to stay only for the weekend, he documented the entire event in exchange for hospitality. This was his introduction to Fluxus and here he made his first public performance. Horobin now danced to the universal tune of 'Monty Cantsin', the open-name Neoist pop star. He co-organised and documented two Neoist Apartment Festivals, 'APT 8', London (1984) and 'APT 9', Ponte Nossa (1985) *The Year of Monty Cantsin*.

As the Neoist Network disintegrated, Horobin retreated into the Scottish landscape, making a series of long distance walks. These were personal pilgrimages, and the DATA which resulted was mailed regularly. In 1988 he worked as artist in residence to Dundee Resource Centre for the Unemployed, establishing an alternative venue and staging *The Festival of Non-Participation*. This decentralised event included 'Home-Taping Evenings', 'Fast Days', 'Walking Weekends', 'Cycle Days', 'Switch-Off TV Days', 'The Alternative Garden Festival', and 'The Burning'.

By 1989 Horobin was mentally and physically prepared for his greatest challenge, *The Year of the Tent*, living outdoors, undertaking long distance walks, and maintaining his correspondence art, preparing daily A4 waterproof DATA sheets detailing internal and external conditions, stenciling the date and completing the twice daily ritual of recording pulse, blood pressure, urinalysis, mood swings and weather. The DATA project terminated somewhere between Iona and Glasgow on 31.12.89.

Peter Haining

# ATTIC DATA

CORRESPONDENCE

**PORTRAIT**

**CORRESPONDENCE**

**PORTRAIT**

# KAREN STRANG

Pete Horobin
Correspondence Portrait, DATA (Daily Action Time Archive)
**1980–90**

Ian Hamilton finlay
First Battle of Little Sparta
**February 4 1983**

'Icy, bleak dawn reveals defence in depth astride the single approach ... "Checkpoint Sandy", named in honour of the Sherrif's Officer Alexander 'Sandy' Walker, stands before the bridge. YOU ARE NOW ENTERING LITTLE SPARTA warns a red and white counterweight barrier reminiscent of the Berlin Wall. The Checkpoint is covered by a camouflaged Mk. IV Panzer ... Minefields stretch as far as the eye can see ...'

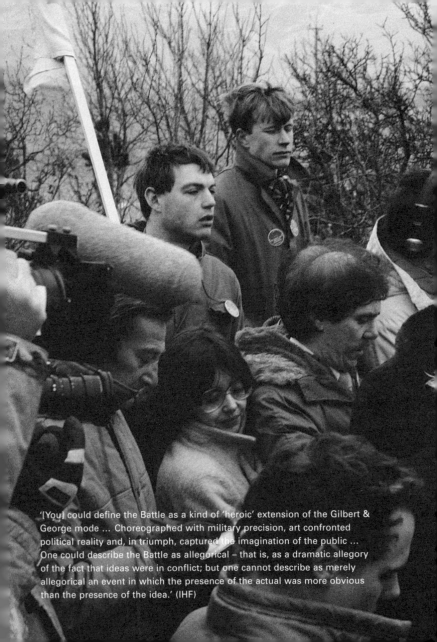

'[You] could define the Battle as a kind of 'heroic' extension of the Gilbert & George mode ... Choreographed with military precision, art confronted political reality and, in triumph, captured the imagination of the public ... One could describe the Battle as allegorical – that is, as a dramatic allegory of the fact that ideas were in conflict; but one cannot describe as merely allegorical an event in which the presence of the actual was more obvious than the presence of the idea.' (IHF)

Back left: Mark Stewart, Andrew Townshend. Centre facing: Sandy Walker

*Strathclyde*
*cosiest state in the U.S.S.R.*

BLACK THE THIRD EYE

JOIN THE
SAINT-JVST
VIGILANTES

ROCKY ITHAKA for Champ

**TODAY THE REGION!
TOMORROW THE WORLD!!**

TO BE A HERO
IT IS NOT ENOUGH
TO WRITE TO BUREAUCRACY TWICE

**NEO-CLASSICISM - THE MARBLE ARROW!**

STRATHCLYDE REGION
DER UNTERGANG DES ABENDLANDES

# Strathclyde
## The Infernal Region

Ian Hamilton Finlay
Rubber stamps from The Little Spartan War

# The Desmoulins Connection

*'Strathclyde Region can only make political statements.'* – Strathclyde Regional Council Press Office, during The Little Spartan War.

News from Strathclyde Region: In Strathclyde where the Authority has direct access to the citizen's bank account, self-locking mattresses are all the rage.

The two excuses of the liberal: It is trivial and not worth worrying about. It is too unpleasant and ought to be ignored.

*'Servility cloaked in affluence. He wears a coloured shirt.'* – Saint-Just Vigilante on John Fowler of the *Glasgow Herald*.

One letter soothes the liberal's conscience. Three hundred letters may actually get something done.

'If he won't have his head in his hands he can have his head in a basket.' – Saint-Just Vigilante on Angus Stirling, Director-General of The National Trust, during the Follies War.

News from Strathclyde Region: The Region is among the official 'advisers' to the Glasgow Garden Festival. Among those not advising are Capability Brown, Humphrey Repton and Alexander Pope.

*'If they had to choose between betraying their country and betraying their cronies, they'd betray their country.'* – Saint-Just Vigilante on The National Trust for Scotland, during the Follies War. (See E. M. Forster.)

Liberty for some, Equality for some, Fraternity with some.

Robespierre was the first, and only, President of France.

'*He is so conceited he wants a War all to himself.*' – Saint-Just Vigilante on Waldemar Januszczak, during the Follies War.

In Liberal democracy the Police may be unarmed but Fashion carries a gun.

Liberal democracy dislikes the association of Virtue and Terror. It finds Virtue offensive.

'*Being attacked by Waldemar is like being guillotined with a turnip.*' – Saint-Just Vigilante on Waldemar Januszczak, art critic of the *Guardian*.

'*Deserters don't like to be reminded that this world is a battlefield.*' – Saint-Just Vigilante on certain liberals who dislike disputes.

'*Don't be overheard saying that violence exists in the universe: you may get shot.*' – Saint-Just Vigilante, after listening to Julian Spalding's radio interview with Ian Hamilton Finlay.

Ian Hamilton Finlay
Published by the Committee of Public Safety, Little Sparta
**1988**

*from* Holy Loch Soap
*I will sing of facts but some will say I invented them.*
(Ovid, 'Metamorphoses')

## US Navy presence (in memoriam) 1961-1991

This soap, of Holy Loch, in Cowal, Argyll, Scotland, records the presence of 5,000 United States nationals (service men and women and their families; sub-contractors and 'servicing agents'). At Holy Loch, the US Navy operated and serviced nuclear submarines and their armed missiles.

Over thirty years, between 75,000 and 150,000 US nationals passed through the town of Dunoon, on the shores of Holy Loch. The figures are vague, since for security reasons no accurate figures have ever been issued by either the US Navy or the MOD. As also there have never been precise figures on number and types of missiles present, accidents, or indeed what remains on the seabed, tangible or otherwise.

**Accident**: in November 1981 a Poseidon missile being winched between the tender and a submarine fell, or as the US Navy put it 'descended at a faster than normal rate'.

**Security**: provided by forty-five US Marines 'who are not well known for their refined behaviour' armed with M16 rifles, pump action shotguns and stun grenades who stood permanent guard behind the heavy steel doors of the nuclear storage area.

**Command**: SSBNs (nuclear-powered attack submarine or 'hunter-killer') rested with the US Navy's Commander-in-Chief Atlantic (CINCLANT) at Norfolk, Virginia, exercising control through Commander-in-Chief US Atlantic Fleet (CINCLANTFLT) and the Commander Submarine Force Atlantic Fleet as part of the US strategic nuclear forces. Under a 1961 agreement, 400 warheads, (two submarines worth) were allocated to NATO's Supreme Allied Commander Europe (SACEUR) who would use them as theatre weapons for 'deep interdiction missions against fixed targets'.

*father hear my confession*
*peace is my profession*

1 (vii)
I set the scene for you

something akin to a proverb hatches
in cockroach cracks
*Pope's men explode*
*Diet of ants*
*Armsdeal signpost*
*Kiss Me Kate*


2
Holy Loch (Loch Striven Loch Ewe
Machrihanish Stornoway Cape Wrath
Thurso Forss Thurso West Murkle Tain
Inverbevie Edzell Rosyth)

*USS Proteus*
*USS Hunley*
*USS Simon Lake*
*USS Canopus*
*USS Holland*
*USS Hunley*
*USS Simon Lake*
                    the ships
Waggle o' the Kilt
                    the show on the promenade

8
Holy Loch Soap
the poor of a nation
to worship I consume
cracker barrel honky tonk honky
wobbling globes of shower flesh
around sphincter enthusiasts
iron pumping head bands
one two one two sweat
dollar droppings scramble
oh clean cut lubrication
collision love violation
ligament featherlite action packed
holy loch assumption spent
consummation cindy
sunshine reverie


10 (ii)
my observation is we
bottle and sell the sun
outbid and liquidate
the long stolen journey

14

glendaruel glen of the
river running red
of columbine and bishopweed
of the rowan oak and alder
of the cupmarked stones
of kilbridemor and kilmodan
ardacheranmor where I talk
in the sun with friends
the mewling buzzard cartwheels
as though the black jet
    like a falling mountain
    that blackly travels ahead of the exploding air
    as fast as my thought
never was
the curlew bubbles and whoops
and the cockerel crows
and the cuckoo
and the echo

where I enter the lyrical
on a need to know basis

*Titan Atlas Thor Navaho Snark*
*Nike-Zeus Mace Bear-A*
*Shyster Scud Blinder Sark*
*Nike-X Blackjack-A*
*Griffon Henhouse Looking Glass Skybolt*

20

time was
when it was all simple
ferns unrolled
outside my old cottage door
umbelliferae I could not name
rosa gallica
bells of columbine
and foxglove
geraniums everywhere
the wild kind
willow herb
all nodded in my direction
I must have been their height
no not childhood
this last flowering explosion
and time disintegrates
numb I wait for new movement
where are the emissaries
the blue flies buzz and batter
at the window
where are the agents of change
who is dreaming me now

Gerry Loose
*Object Permanence* magazine
**1987**

# 16th, 17th, 18th, 19th December 1998

Cruise: A Wandering Voyage In Search Of An Enemy

David Bellingham
A definition to mark four nights of airstrikes in the Gulf, published by WAX366
1998

David Bellingham's WAX366 press is one of a number of fugitive small presses run by writers and artists. Others include Wild Hawthorn Press (Ian Hamilton Finlay), Moschatel Press (Thomas A. & Laurie Clark), Byways Press (Gerry Loose), Weproductions (Helen Douglas and Telfer Stokes), Armpit Press (David Shrigley), Morning Star (Alec Finlay), *Rebel Inc.* magazine (Kevin Williamson) and other magazines such as *Object Permanence* (Peter Manson and Robin Purves), *atopia* (Gavin Morrison & Fraser Stables), and *Depression News* (S. B. Kelly).

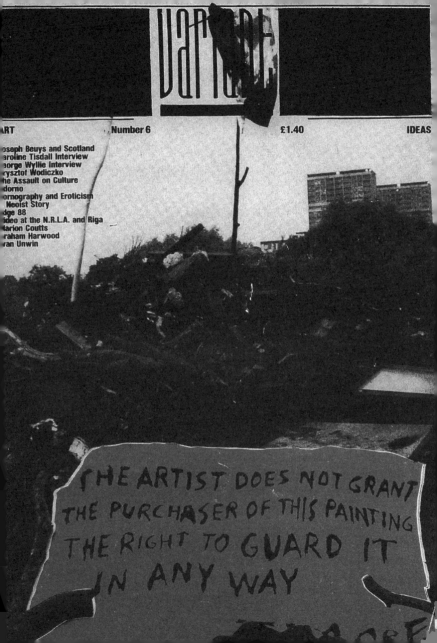

ART      Number 6      £1.40      IDEAS

THE ARTIST DOES NOT GRANT
THE PURCHASER OF THIS PAINTING
THE RIGHT TO GUARD IT
IN ANY WAY

# FESTIVAL OF PLAGIARISM

## A COLLECTIVE VISION

PLAGIARISM is the conscious manipulation of pre-existing elements in the creation of 'aesthetic' works. Plagiarism is inherent in all 'artistic' activity, since both pictorial and literary 'arts' function with an inherited language; even when their practitioners aim at overthrowing this received syntax (as happened with modernism and post-modernism).

At the beginning of the twentieth century, the way in which pre-existing elements were used in 'artistic' productions underwent a quantitative leap with the 'discovery' of collage. This development was pre-figured in the 'writings' of Isidore Ducasse (1846–1870), who is better known by his pen name 'Lautreamont'. In his 'poems', Ducasse wrote: "Plagiarism is necessary. Progress implies it." This maxim summarises the use to which plagiarism has been put ever since. Two, or more , divergent elements are brought together to create new meanings. The resulting sum is greater than the individual parts.

The lettristes, and later the situationists, called this process 'detournement' (diversion is a literal translation from the french), but the activity is still popularly known as plagiarism – the term that Lautreamont used.

Plagiarism enriches human language, it is a collective undertaking far removed from the post-modern 'theories' of appropriation. Plagiarism implies a sense of history and leads to progressive social transformation. In contrast, the 'appropriations' of post-modern ideologists are individualistic and alienated. Plagiarism is for life, post-modernism is fixated on death.

# FROM ORIGINALITY TO ONTOLOGY

# THE DECLINE OF THE TEXT

# GLASGOW AUGUST 198

# Beechgrove Garden Festival

*(Alec and Dougal potter about with watering cans, trowels, etc. Centre stage, a floral sheet or cloth covers two more figures. Dougal looks up and addresses the audience.)*

**Dougal:** Oh, Hullo!

**Alec:** *(also taking note of audience)* Hullo, there!

**Dougal:** Hullo and welcome to the Beechgrove Garden Roadshow. And today, Alec and I are in ... Where the fuck are we, Alec?

**Alec:** Well, today we're in a verra big garden indeed, Dougal.

**Dougal:** Fuckin' enormous garden, Alec.

**Alec:** That's right, Dougal, because today we're at the Glasgow Garden Festival. And isn't it miraculous?

**Dougal:** Aye, aye. Whit's miraculous, Alec?

**Alec:** It's miraculous tae find a Garden festival in a major industrial centre sicas Glasgow, Dougal?

**Dougal:** Aye. For example, Alec, vit's that over there?

**Alec:** Well, that's whit we cry a green belt, Dougal. Parkheid. And it's right next door tae that lovely red, white and blue display, Brigtonus Masonicus, with that provocative wee splash of UDA over in the corner, look.

**Dougal:** Lovely, but for me Alec, this is where it all began, here at Queen's Dock in Govan.

**Alec:** Aye, well you know what they say Dougal – flowers are a lot prettier than cranes.

**Dougal:** Aye, and the great thing about flowers, of course, is that they keep coming back, year after year. But once the cranes and the ships and the jobs have gone, they never seem to come back, do they?

**Alec:** Verra true, but I've got a wee surprise for ye here tae cheer us all up.

**Dougal:** Vit's that, Alec?

**Alec:** Well *(Alec whips the sheet off the 'display', which consists of a yuppie in a bowler hat, with a briefcase and tennis racquet clutched nervously to his person, and a suspicious worker)*, it's this we growth of Bourgie Obnoxicus, right here in Govan.

**Dougal:** Lovely.

**Alec:** Oh, he doesn't look too happy, Dougal, I'm afraid.

**Dougal:** We'd better get right down tae work here, Alec, it looks like.

**Alec:** Aye. On ye go then. *(Alec explains while Dougal pokes ate the plants).* Ye see, the thing aboot yer 'Wee Yuppy', as we gardeners affectionately cry him, is that they're a fragile, delicate sort o' plantie. They're never completely happy until they're entirely surrounded by plants like themselves.

**Dougal:** So, in order for your 'Wee Yuppy' tae flourish in a new area like Govan, we've got tae get rid of the hardier, not quite so nice 'Proletarian Skintibus', or 'Scum', as we gardeners call them. So, first of aw, we pull oot aw the weeds *(removes his fag)*, then *(watering him from the can)*, we let the water seep intae the living areas, and when they call the council tae dry them oot *(drags him to far side of the stage)* we repot them way, way over here in this dry, arid, desert region we gardeners cry Drumchapel.

*(Yuppie, now with more room, gets happier, plays tennis, mixes cocktails, etc.)*

And if he tries tae come back, he'll find the area has been completely overrun by Bourgie Obnoxicus. This is the process known tae us as Barretting.

**Alec:** And tae the District Council, the area has been Laffertied.

**Dougal:** Or fucked up completely.

**Alec:** So here's yer new Glasgow. All the Scum chucked out on tae the Compost Schemes, and lots of pretty flowers and obnoxious yuppies, everywhere ye look.

**Dougal:** Remember, Alec, how in the old days we had tae wait for the scum tae work themsels tae death before we could get rid of them.

**Alec:** That's the wonders of the Scottish Development Agency for ye, Dougal. Cos ye know what they say?

**Alec & Dougal:** GLASGOW'S MILES BETTER ... for yer wee yuppies.

*(Yuppie whinnies in agreement, and the worker looks on.)*

END.

Peter Arnott & Peter Mullan
Sketch performed by Red Heads: Arnott, Mullan, Kate Donnely, and Libby MacArthur; first published in *Worker's City*, edited by Farquhar MacLay, Clydeside Press
**1988**

# Red Clyde

In 1988, I spent a year on the Fullbright Exchange Programme teaching at the University of Illinois near Chicago. Whilst in Chicago, I was entranced to see the river dyed green for St Patrick's Day . . .

When proposals were invited for the Glasgow Garden Festival in 1988, I began to think about the possibility of dyeing the River Clyde red. There were several associations for me: of course the first was the 'Red Clyde' of the 1910's and 20's. Between June 1915 and March 1916 a rent strike was organised in Glasgow. It was essentially a women's fight with many of the male householders being away at war. The rents had been increased because of demand for accommodation for munitions workers. Eighteen women were taken to court and 10,000 protested. Fearing a General Strike, the government passed the Rent Restrictions Act to prevent large rent increases. Women received the vote in 1918.

The second was the relationship between rivers (the life-blood of cities) and the human body with its veins and arterial structure.

The proposal was not realised, but maybe one day . . .

Sam Ainsley
Proposal for Glasgow Garden Festival
**1988**

"The European Cultcha Capital notion was started by Melina Mercouri, the Greek minista fo aats. Athens hade been stone-cleaned, she wanted tourists to know it, she suggested to Brussels that Athens be the first cultcha capital, then otha countries could have a shot. Nobody objected. Italy chose Florence; the Nethalands, Amstadam; Germany, Berlin; France predictably chose Paris. But Being Cultcha Capital is expensive. You must advatise yawself. Put on extra show and consats. Invite foreign guests. Stage boring receptions. Margaret Thatcha isn't keen on all that crap; anyway London has enough of it. Like a sensible monetarist she put the job up fo grabs and offad it to the lowest bidda. Bath and Edinburgh put in fo it, Cardiff, Birmingham and Glasgow: but only Glasgow gave a quiet little promise that if it got the job it would not ask the central govament fo cash. So Glasgow, which the Lay-ba Party has ruled fo ova half a century, was given the job by the Tory arts minista who announced that Glasgow had set an example of independent action which should be followed by every local authority in the United Kingdom. Wia funding the entaprize out of the rates and public propaty sales and sponsaship from banks, oil companies, building societies and whateva we can screw out of Europe.

"And Glasgow deserves the job! It's the headquartas of the Scottish Opera, Scottish Ballet, Scottish National Orchestra, the Burrell Collection, the Citizen's Theata, the Third Eye Centa and an intanational drama festival: all of them directed and mostly administered by the English, of course. Sometimes the natives get a bit bolshie about it but I'm very firm with them. I say very quietly, 'Listen! You Scots have been expoating yaw own people to England and everywha else fo centuries, and nobody has complained much about you! Why start howling just because wia giving you a taste of yaw own medicine?' They can't think of an ansa to that one."

"But shooali the natives have some local cultcha of tha own?" says the dealer, "What about these young paintas who've emerged? Campbell and Currie etcetera."

"The ones who did well in New Yawk? Yes, we'll put them on a show."

"Has Glasgow nothing else apart form Billy Connolly?"

"Some novels by Glasgow writas have had rave reviews in *The Times* Lit. Sup., but I'm afraid they leave me cold. Half seem to be written in phonetic Scotch about people with names like Auld Shug. Every second word seems to be fuck, though hardly any fucking happens. Tha otha half have complicated plots like SM obstacle races in which I entie-aly lose my way and give up. As a matta of fact, Harry, I have one of these books hia to give to you! Some of it reminded me of games we once played with Hijordis."

Alasdair Gray
**1990**

Mark Pawson & Roddy Buchanan paste-up of Ross Sinclair's 'Capital of Culture/Culture of Capital', Dublin. Simultaneous pastings took place in Amsterdam and Glasgow.
**1990**

Craig Richardson
London
February 2002

September 2001. Before a hundred hours had passed since the air attack on the World Trade Centre two Scottish artists sat on a sleek bench in Dundee Contemporary Art discussing their works' related but subjective elimination at Aberdeen Art Gallery from the survey exhibition 'Here + Now'. I overheard one, Kenny Hunter, say to the other, Christine Borland, 'there needs to be a politically engaged art.' Censorious Aberdeen Officials – Take Heed. Summer 2001 at Transmission Gallery and it's under attack from the press and maybe the Council. A justifiably defensive press release tells its members that it once had a radical past, supporting groups such as Workers City. What it cannot spell out is that such affiliations resulted in public performances of a play by James Kelman and a collaborative exhibition involving Euan Sutherland and Ross Sinclair which influenced the direction of the latter's future work.

As an archaeologist brushes back the layers of the present to sink into the past I looked back and found these moments. These are moments where doubt is expressed and where a shift in my cultural perception may have taken place. Early 2001, with the curator of 'Circles' at Z. K. M. Karlsruhe, Claire Barclay, Roderick Buchanan, Jacqueline Donachie, Martin Boyce, Simon Starling, Toby Paterson, Nathan Coley, myself and others discussed the possible reasons why some artists declined to join us in the exhibition. 'Was it the invitation to play football?' (which had come with the invitation to exhibit) suggested the curator. Could it be some artists did not make art, in 'response' to the idea of friendship and identity as a group of Glasgow-based artists. Ironically, in 1991, one of these non-attendees, Cathy Wilkes, had fallen off some ladders and the exhibition 'Speed' was devised as a replacement for her, now physically impossible, programmed exhibition at Transmission Gallery. Invitations to participate were sent on Saturday and almost all replied affirmatively by the following Monday.

In 1997 Kirsty Ogg escaped from Norwich, set up shop at The Showroom Gallery near my local in London's East End, and exhibited the latest work of Jim Lambie, David Allen, Claire Barclay and others. When I visited the exhibitions I believed I may have been seeing the first real Transmission Gallery 'franchise'. Scots abroad. In 1995–6 I often met with Graham Fagen when we worked in the Midlands. We sustained ourselves with the mantra of 'Scotia Nostra' – used to describe a situation in the Seventies when a number of English Art Courses were headed by Scots. Graham's art flourished when he returned home to Glasgow, and I enjoy receiving his invitation cards at regular intervals.

1994. Artists meet in Tramway and explain to the selectors of 'The British Art Show 1995' that coming to Scotland for just a day, was not sufficient, not anymore. But thinking back to the Summer of 1991 a large number of European artists exhibited alongside an equal number of Scottish artists in 'Windfall'. What did we learn from the European artists? Nothing, I have long suspected, as have others. But an outstanding publication was produced by Tony Arefin. For a significant period he was the major publisher and subsidiser of Scottish art publications, whose unhappy death in 2000 ends the 1990s as far as I am concerned.

Early 1991. The Gulf War, Operation Desert Storm ends with the mass slaughter of retreating Iraqi conscripts . Isn't one of art's jobs to re-imagine that Road to Basra?

In 1989 an exhibition 'Information' opened at Paisley Art Gallery and Museum. The title subconsciously emulated the seminal 1970 exhibition in New York's Museum of Modern Art. The 1989 exhibition had an undeniable conceptual undertone. It instilled such a poor response from the Museum Director that he closed the exhibition early. The follow-up to 'Information', 'Incorporate', was devised as a series of artistic interventions along the corridors and up the Carrara marble staircases of Glasgow's City Chambers. In order to develop this, three young artists went to an appointment with Clerks of the City Chambers. The officials put their foot down on the proposals of approximately thirty artists. Shamefully retreating in our suits, confidence badly dented, the three of us were aghast. Later, amid desperate laughter in a George Square cafe, looking out on a damp vista, we said: 'Fuck them'.

In 1988 Douglas Gordon and myself sent a rolled-up poster, which announced our forthcoming performance, to Richard Demarco. On the spur of the moment we filled the tube with sawdust, in the hope he would open the tube above his typewriter and wonder who these sneaky people were. Allegedly, three years later we would confess to a curator from the Jack Tilton Gallery, to her genuine horror, that maybe we had taken a small amount of earth from Walter De Maria's 'New York Earth Room'. Maybe this earth lay unclaimed, through the 1990s, in some Glasgow flat, before crumbling into dust.

In 1990 Glen Onwin gave me a copy of his newly published book *Recovery of Dissolved Surfaces*. This book, suffused, as with much art from the Seventies, with an Arte Povera style particularly in its homage to Beuys, seems more timely than ever. It has an ecological approach and scientific-documentary aesthetic. Why did he stop this research? The book now sits on my shelves alongside the catalogue for 'Graeme Murray Gallery at The Serpentine'. The publication notes that Ken Dingwall had a number of exhibitions in Graeme's gallery, in June 1977, in December 1979, and was included in a group exhibition in June 1980. He is also included in the exhibition ' New Works in Contemporary Art' which happens at the Orchard Gallery, Derry. Ken Dingwall? I know he lives in Ohio now, but where is he?

Some time before, Donald Judd speaks at the Fruitmarket Gallery, rigorously, for three hours to an audience of six hundred, discussing his work's dimensions and his sense of betrayal at the mismanagement of his collected works. Sam Ainsley casts a weary eye at the surroundings of this talk – they do not answer her anxiety over her participation in 'The Vigorous Imagination'. She has serious misgivings about the exhibition sponsors, Shell UK Ltd. She advocates withdrawal by all the artists, including Ken Currie and Peter Howson, but finds a 'solution' later, through Nancy Spero and Leon Golub's answer to her question, 'should she exhibit in an exhibition sponsored by Shell?' They reply that a work's political effect is undiminished by its context (see Saatchi Collection). Her anxiety and misgivings do not go away but her attentions are drawn to the increasing demands of her students, who feel like accomplices in her conscientious, politicised approach. At the Opening of 'The Vigorous Imagination' a generation of artists meet Donald Dewar and offer him some sweets. Later, appalled by the slackness in concept of 'The Vigorous Imagination', Graeme Murray suggests a title for a new exhibition, 'The Rigorous Imagination'.

I am surprised that anyone should be invited to contribute an essay to a proposed anthology which addressed 'political concerns'. Now more than ever, Scottish art has an unambiguous international dimension and broad international presence. From the perspective of 2001 looking back into the last decade I see that orthodoxy and peer pressure in Scottish visual art has been potentially oppressive, pulling some artists away from the precipice of political concerns. The withdrawal of institutional support for *Variant* under the editorship of Malcolm Dickson consigned much of these concerns to the margins of cultural visibility. That remains for me the central shift away from what *could* have been, in Scottish visual art in the Nineties. In many ways it heralded a period of uncritical celebration. Malcolm was mindful to promote and document such activities as artist run spaces (including Transmission Gallery and others such as Pictorial Heroes and Billy Clark) and socially or publicly sited artworks, as well as being forward-thinking enough to develop the New Visions Video Festival.

To understand the *now* in Scottish art we must also peer into the unknown Seventies. A light-absorbent surface of matt black appears before me. Held in there is the atmosphere of the three-day week and Heath's government ingloriously falling, through to the period of the 'failed' Devolution vote at the end of the Seventies. Then, regret: Margaret. Retreat, Failure, Defeat. The easing of the Scottish licensing laws are also particularly important. (I cannot place why but there remains an anxiety about alcohol and failure in Scottish culture. But what about failure to get through the dim winters? Or existential failure?). The history of this formative time reverberates from the concerns I have now: the history of contemporary Scottish art; Edinburgh Ceramic Workshop and how it was wound up (its remaining bank balance became an artwork in its own right, with an irredemptive possibility that it would one day break the world's banks); the never-ending Fruitmarket Gallery; Richard Demarco and his tussles with The Scottish Arts Council; and on and on . . .

Cultural significance does not just reside with the youngest but with cross-generational discussion. During the 1990s artists sought the critical assistance of James Kelman, Thomas Lawson, Murdo MacDonald, Alan Johnston, and others, seeking not only kind acts, supportive words and invitations to open spaces, but also the resemblance of an authoritative voice, even one which could be rejected and then rediscovered. This happened with David Harding at Glasgow School of Art and his influential Environmental Art course. But it is the continuous affliction of Scottish culture that the voice should be divided.

I could write a whole letter on the fundamentally different atmosphere of the 1990s from that of its predecessors just with reference to the dynamism of the many female artists who continued to exert such a strong identity on the decade. Somebody has to do this at some point. Fairness of approach is the most animating form of criticism and I am urged to write from a personal, and no doubt unfair, perspective.

I have doubts about the lessons of a cultural history my peers and those younger than I can learn. The 1990s were a time when Scottish artists could move forward, away from their predecessors' concerns, the official history of recent decades having neither served them well nor found a way to acknowledge their presence until it was too late. It is also possible that, culturally and politically, change was enacted with reference to England – not because of but in spite of – more than we may consider to be the case. We have arrived at the Aftermath. As I write in London and edit my memories, I also read of successful moves in Scotland to confront the needs of the uneducated, the sick, the defenceless in ways which differ from policies enacted by Westminster. But as I write I must also contain some personal anxiety at the assertion: there is no going back.

Craig Richardson

Douglas Gordon, *Proof*
Installation to commemorate civil uprisings, Glasgow Green
**1990**

Noam Chomsky
Public lecture 'Self-Determination & Power' event
Pierce Institute, Govan
**1990**

# Self-Determination & Power

<u>Revised Draft Proposal</u>

DATES: 10 January 1990  LOCATION: Pearce Institute, Govan

Organised and Supported by:
*Edinburgh Review* - (to be confirmed)
Free University
*Scottish Child* magazine

Self-determination in the world is a universal task. How does the individual establish self in the group/institution/society? How do groups with common interests achieve their goals in their political context?

This jointly run event will, from the keynote contribution by American radical critic, Noam Chomsky, look at the task of self-determination in the contemporary Scottish context.

<u>Proposed programme</u>

<u>Wed 10th January</u>

| | |
|---|---|
| 9.30–10.30 | Registration and coffee |
| 10.30–11.00 | Opening remarks / setting the context / Organisation |
| 11.00–12.30 | <u>Self-determination: a life task, a political task</u><br>Noam Chomsky (45–50 minutes) |
| | Remarks and thoughts in reply by one or two commentators with specific reference to the Scottish context: |

> James Kelman )
> Derek Rodger ) one to chair
> female speaker )

| | |
|---|---|
| 12.30–1.45 | LUNCH (Catering on the premises) |
| 1.45–3.15 | Discussion groups |

Maximum 15 groups of maximum 20 people.

Each group will be led by an event member designated by the event management. The task of the workshop group will be to study  through members' own experience, the possibilities for, and obstacles to self-determined action in Scotland.

| 3.15 | Coffee/tea |
| 3.45–4.30 | Plenary Panel discussion – Noam Chomsky and others. |
| 4.30–7.30 | No Programme – bar open, bookstalls, displays |
| 7.30–12.00 | Readings and Concert – programme to be worked out in outline |

OPTIONAL and/or SEPARATE EVENT

Thursday 11th January

2.00–4.00 Optional/Separate Seminar held in Pearce Institute OR other venue

Noam Chomsky and others on a philosophical theme

4.00–4.30 Coffee/Tea

4.30–7.30 Bar/Bookstalls/Displays

7.30–12.00 Readings and Concert

An invited membership will comprise about one third of the participants. These will include: 15 workshop group leaders; a number of Scottish writers, critics, and commentators; a similar group from furth of Scotland; about 30 (2 per workshop) people who have made great efforts at determination. These could include: members of community action groups, tenants groups, anti-dampness in housing campaigners, women's groups, ethnic rights groups, the peace movement/anti-nuclear campaigners, workers' cop-ops, youth groups etc.

All writers and musicians attending will be invited to perform/read in the evening event(s).

The remainder of the membership will be drawn up by application through publicity.

10 January 1990

# Cabaret Programme
# for the 1993 Season in the Auld Howff

## JULY

| | |
|---|---|
| Friday 29th | Dick and Lillie. |
| Saturday 30th | Dessie, Dick and Lillie. |

## AUGUST

| | |
|---|---|
| Friday 5th | Dick and Lillie. |
| Saturday 6th | Dessie. |
| Sunday 7th | PartyNite including Darts and Bingo. |
| Friday 12th | Tibetan Nomad Fancy Dress Nite. |
| Saturday 13th | Dick. |
| Friday 17th | Family Nite with Medieval Bouncy Castle. |
| Saturday 18th | Dick and Dessie. |
| Monday 20th | Elvis Presley in Concert. |
| Friday 24th | Lillie, Dick and Dessie. |
| Saturday 25th | How to Build a Stone Dyke, an Outdoor Activity starting at 6am. |

## SEPTEMBER

| | |
|---|---|
| Saturday 1st | Dick, Lillie and Dessie. |
| Sunday 2nd | Zulu Fancy Dress Nite |
| Monday 3rd | Lillie. |
| Friday 7th | Scottish Family Nite sponsored by Minnigaff TV Satellite Systems. |
| Saturday 8th | Dick, Dessie and Lillie. |
| Sunday 9th | Dick, Dessie and Surprise Guest. |
| Monday 10th | Secrets of Home Baking by the Creetown Obese Society. |
| Friday 14th | Lillie and Dick's Farewell Party. |
| Saturday 15th | (Private Party – Staff Only.) |

Brent Hodgson
Clocktower Press booklet no. 7
1992

# Uniform Feelings

jenerilly speekn
wimmin huv this thing
aboot men
in yooniforums

thay wonty
UNDRESS thum

this iz troo
ah hate that yooniforum shit
GET THUM OAFF!

Alison Flett
Clocktower Press booklet no. 8
**1993**

Produced by Duncan McLean in South Queensferry, Clocktower Press published ten booklets (1990–96) featuring the work of little known young Scottish writers, including James Meek, Alan Warner and Irvine Welsh.

As

sky

falls

into global muff
wrapped around in melanin,
tans in fax of fuzz box,
there's mud in your lie,
are you feared of creatures
such as that slunk yawn of

art thou slow dancing,

unprepared to leave
space for air beneath
the flow of bodies,
whisked to viper for
the hair you breathe,
clasping your untipped

furry

tongue.

# NO

WAY, NO SNAKE BITE,

just forked tongue
on doggy brek,
get that down you,
pic 'n' mix
herbaceous borders
freshed off balkan
smorgasbord,

# OH

but it does you good
to go suck tartan,

weight off your pins,
as the clutch goes off
the risus purus, chocs
and spleen away, count-
down and LEFT OFF!
to the end of our common

# ERA.

Drew Milne
from *How Peace Came*
1994

# Leonard's Shorter Catechism

*"And now would you please welcome St Augustine of Hippo, who's come along this evening to talk about 'The Concept of the Just Fuel-Air-Explosive Bomb'."*

Q What is meant by the phrase 'by peaceful means'?

A 'By peaceful means' is a special United Nations phrase meaning 'No food or medicine to be allowed in' to a country. If for instance Iraq, Palestine and Cuba had a disagreement with Great Britain and we were able to blockade the country from receiving any food or medicine, this would be called 'pursuing their disagreement with Great Britain by peaceful means'.

Q Why did Pope Urban the Second launch the First Crusade?

A 'To restore peace and stability in the Middle East'.

Q Who said 'Blessed are the meek: for they shall inherit the earth'?

A This was said by Jesus Christ on the Mount of Olives. He was quoting in anticipation George Bush, who used the words in his address to the American people after ordering the mass bombing of Iraq.

Q What flies from Gloucestershire?

A This might be any one of a number of migratory birds of Gloucestershire which winter on the Mediterranean or Africa. For example, the Garden Warbler, the Nightjar, the Swift, the Stonechat, or the Whinchat with its snappy *tic-tac* and soft *peu*, and its 5–7 pale blue eggs laid in a cupped surface on the ground under shrubbery.

Q What do you call something that flies from Gloucestershire to a place where it 'minces everything on the ground within an area one mile wide by three miles long'?

A  A human being.

Q  What do you call the things that mince everything on the ground within an area one mile wide by three miles long?

A  'Conventional weapons'.

Q  What flies across France?

A  Only birds, planes, human beings and conventional weapons are allowed to fly across France.

Q  Sphinx: What goes on four legs in the morning, two legs in the afternoon, and three legs in the evening?

A  American pilot: 'A cockroach'.

Q  What is the percentage of people in command of the British Army who have working-class accents?

A  I'm sorry, he *would* have been pleased to speak to you, but he is in bed with laryngitis.

Q  What is the percentage of British troops in the front line who have public-school accents?

A  I'm sorry, he *would* have been pleased to speak to you, but he is in bed with laryngitis.

Q  What do you get after three weeks if you lock a million-and-a-half people up for 24 hours a day?

A  Thirteen billion dollars.

Q  What did the Scottish National Party say when Iraq annexed Kuwait?

A  'It's Scotland's oil!'

Q  Pete asks: 'If Marconi invented the radio, and Winston Churchill invented Kuwait, who invented the steam engine?'

A  James Watt. And he was Scottish.

Q  What is the etymology of the words 'Saudi Arabia'?

A  'Saudi Arabia' is an abbreviation from an ancient Arabic phrase which translates literally as 'The Aramco Oil Company International'.

Q  In which book does Biggles have a dogfight with the Airforce of the World Enemy, thus helping to save the world at great personal risk?

A  *Biggles Goes to War, Biggles Flies South, Biggles Flies North*, etc.

Q  In which book does the Airforce of the World Enemy run away, so Biggles bombs cities, towns, roads, bridges, telephone exchanges, water supplies and electricity supplies, so that the survivors have difficulty getting treatment?

A  *The Minutes of the British War Cabinet January–February 1991.*

Q  What did the Labour Shadow Cabinet say when it realised it was an essential part of a Government of National Unity waging planned genocide?

A  Shhh.

Q   What did you used to call someone who should feel guilty about their country's past policy of genocide?

A   A German.

Q   What do you call a quarter of a million Germans marching in 1991 against genocide?

A   'Anti-semitic'.

Q   What do you do when a president gasses 5,000 people in his own country?

A   Show the bodies on television – but keep selling him arms.

Q   What do you do when a president's troops invade Panama killing another 5,000 people?

A   Don't show the bodies on television.

Q   What does 'control of the airwaves' mean?

A   It means suspending oil adverts until people can watch them and keep their food down at the same time.

A   The telephones sell-off, the gas sell-off, the water sell-off, the electricity sell-off, the Tory leadership contest, the total destruction of Iraq . . .

Q   What is the question?

Q   What did Britain take part in on Tuesday, February 19th 1991?

A   It took part in what was at that point 'one of the most ferocious attacks on the centre of Baghdad', using bombers and Cruise Missiles fired from ships.

Q   **What did John Major say about the bombing the next day?**

A   He said: 'One is bound to ask about attacks such as these: What sort of people is it that can carry them out? They certainly are consumed with hate. They are certainly sick of mind, and they can be certain of one thing – they will be hunted and hunted until they are found.' (He was talking about 5lb of explosive left in a litter-bin at Victoria Station in London. This killed one person and critically injured three.)

Q   **'Many of these modern weapons show a considerable amount of imagination in their construction. I was told the other day that some rockets can each saturate an area the size of 60 football pitches. Is this true?'**

A   'Yes! They're fired from multiple-rocket-launch systems, and twelve can be fired at a time. Every rocket breaks up into 600 smaller bombs or 'bomblets' before they land. They're sometimes jocularly called 'the honourable members' after the honourable members of the British House of Commons that voted for the war. You could maybe have a think about *that* next time you're watching Prime Minister's Question Time on TV!'

Q   **What does 'I will only continue to support the war if it stays within United Nations guidelines' mean?**

A  It means 'I support the mass bombing and total destruction of Iraq but I do not support the sending in of armed human beings.'

Q  **What does United Nations Resolution 242 state?**

A  Shhh.

Q  **What do you do with wee babies, four-year-olds, five-year-olds, grannies, people whom you would get on with fine if you know them, people who would get on your nerves, football supporters, teachers, tradesmen, shopkeepers, writers, unemployed people, people that work with their hands, people that work with pens or computers, janitors, directors of firms, managers, people that work at home, bus drivers, taxi drivers, actors, electricians, policemen, clergy, workaholics, feckless wasters, boys out of school into uniform, older soldiers, musicians, alcoholics, geniuses, idiots, people who don't like the light being turned off at night, people who 'prefer the old ways', people who whistle in the street?**

A  Ehm … What country are they from?

*(et cetera, ad infinitum)*

Tom Leonard
**1991**

These 'Questions and Answers on the Gulf War' were completed at the time of the end of the bombing on February 28th, 1991 and first published by AK Press. Since its inception in 1991, AK Press has been the foremost political and counter-cultural press in Scotland, publishing and distributing books and audio CDs. PO Box 12766, Edinburgh EH8 9YE

# thee data base

τηισ τιμε τηε ρεωολυτιον ωιλλ βε διγιτισεδ

**the life of wilhelm reich
oklahoma conspiracies
autonomous astronauts
the out of order order
junkmail backlash
treason in the park**

**issue six / summer 1995 C.E.
published free
by thee data collectiv**

KILL THE CRIMINAL JUSTICE BILL
THE TORIES ARE THE REAL CRIMINALS

KILL THE CRIMINAL JUSTICE BILL
THE TORIES ARE THE REAL CRIMINALS

## knowing is not enough

Alternative fanzine published by Thee Data Collective, based in Glasgow.
1995

SUSPEND YOUR DISBELIEF AS...
THE SOCIETY FOR THE TERMINATION OF ART

# LEVITATE THE GLASGOW GALLERY OF MODERN ART

FORMERLY STIRLINGS LIBRARY AT ROYAL EXCHANGE SQUARE
**FRIDAY, 29th MARCH 1996**
**MIDNIGHT!**

The Society for the Termination of Art protested outside GoMA on the night before it opened. They also mounted a protest at the first Glasgow Art Fair.
**1996**

'The jury's still out on ecstasy. Maybe people will fuck up on it, you don't know. It's so longitudinal, you can't tell. Maybe there's big tumours on the brain ready to burst through like fucking Scanners, or something like that. But eh … one of these things is like, do you want to live forever. If you want to live forever, I think it's a fucking noble sentiment, you know what I mean?'

Irvine Welsh, 'The Ecstasy Interview', *Rebel Inc.*, Issue 4
**1993**

PURE
**The Hogmanay
Party**

**The Fruitmarket**
Merchant City, Glasgow

PUSH presents on saturday night
**Navin
Saunderson**
plus the Pure DJ Squad
**Friday 5th February**

The 7th Birthday Party
ANDREW WEATHERALL
CHEZ DAMIER
TWITCH & BRAINSTORM
& THE BILL

november
ANDREW WEATHERALL

www.ren-com.com/pure

PURE
**1990–2000**

David Shrigley
1995

LEISURE CENTRE

FUUUUUUUUUCK!

DEAD BEATLE$

GRANT MORRI$ON • WRITER
STEVE YEOWELL • ART1$T

DANIEL VOZZO • COLORS
ELECTRIC CRAYON • COLOR SEPARAT1ONS
CLEM ROBIN$ • LETTERS
JOLIE ROTTENBERG • AS$T. EDITOR
STUART MOORE • EDITOR

THE INVISIBLES
CREATED BY GRANT MORRI$ON

*The Invisibles*, Issue no. 1
*The Invisibles* follows the activities of an occult anarcho-terrorist group.
1994

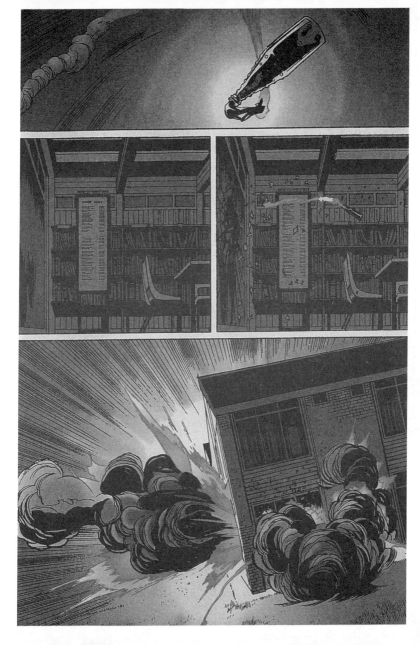

*the curve of Dumgoyach*

the rainbow's arc

and touching both

the summit's pines

Carbeth Huts
Rent Strike 1997 after 40% rent increase.
Poem by Gerry Loose (resident), photograph by Morven Gregor.
**1920–2002**

Alexander & Susan Maris
'Artist with AK47'
**1995**

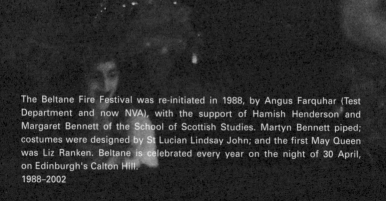

The Beltane Fire Festival was re-initiated in 1988, by Angus Farquhar (Test Department and now NVA), with the support of Hamish Henderson and Margaret Bennett of the School of Scottish Studies. Martyn Bennett piped; costumes were designed by St Lucian Lindsay John; and the first May Queen was Liz Ranken. Beltane is celebrated every year on the night of 30 April, on Edinburgh's Calton Hill.
1988–2002

Beltane Fire Festival
1997

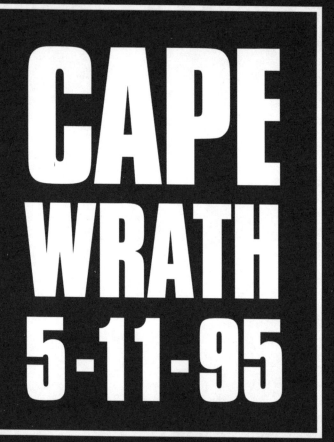

DIVIDED & CREATED

ON 5 NOVEMBER 1995, JIMMY CAUTY & BILL DRUMMOND SIGNED A CONTRACT WITH THE REST OF THE WORLD
AGREEING TO END THE K FOUNDATION FOR A PERIOD OF 23 YEARS

# CAPE
# WRATH
# 5 - 11 - 95

THIS POSTPONEMENT PROVIDES OPPORTUNITY OF SUFFICIENT LENGTH FOR AN ACCURATE AND APPROPRIATELY
EXECUTED RESPONSE TO THEIR 'BURNING OF A MILLION QUID'. THE K FOUNDATION'S FATE NOW LIES IRREVOCABLY
SEALED IN THE IMPLODED REMAINS OF A NISSAN BLUEBIRD NESTLING AMONGST THE ROCKS
600 FEET BELOW CAPE WRATH, SCOTLAND.

8PM TONIGHT, THE PREMIER CARPARK, BRICK LANE

# WHY DID THE K FOUNDATION BURN A MILLION QUID?

**WAS IT A CRIME?**

**WAS IT A BURNT OFFERING?**

**WAS IT MADNESS?**

**WAS IT AN INVESTMENT?**

**WAS IT ROCK 'N' ROLL?**

**WAS IT AN OBSCENITY?**

**WAS IT ART?**

**WAS IT A POLITICAL STATEMENT?**

**WAS IT BOLLOCKS?**

THERE WILL BE SCREENINGS OF THE FILM 'WATCH THE K FOUNDATION BURN A MILLION QUID' AT RELEVANT LOCATIONS OVER THE NEXT TWELVE MONTHS. EACH WILL BE FOLLOWED BY A DEBATE ATTENDED BY MESSRS CAUTY AND DRUMMOND WHERE THE ANSWERS TO THE ABOVE QUESTIONS AND OTHERS WILL BE SOUGHT.

Tara Babel
'streetworks', an international festival
of interventionist live art (Glasgow)
**1998**

**Aberdeenshire**
Capt. A. Farquharson's Invercauld Trusts: 87,500 acres
National Trust for Scotland: 73,582 acres
Viscount Cowdray & Trust: 65,600 acres
The Queen and Trustees of Balmoral: 50,370 acres
Glen Tanar Trusts: 29,150 acres
Capt. A. Ramsay: 25,143 acres
Edward Humphrey and the Westercoull Trust: 23,800 acres
Trustees of Tillypronie Trust: 15,000 acres
Candacraig Trust: 14,000 acres
Sir Ian Okeovar-Walker Bt.: 13,000  acres
BMF Group: 11,700 acres
John Howard Seton Gordon of Abergeldie: 10,200 acres
Alan McLean: 8,460 acres
Trustees of Aberdeen Endowments Trust: 8,008 acres
Donald H. M. and Andrew M. L. Farquharson: 7,900 acres
Sir Andrew G. Forbes-Leith Bt. and family: 7,720 acres
Sir Richard Sutton Settled Estate: 7,574 acres
Frogmore Investments Ltd: 7,300 acres
Georgina Tulloch: 7,200 acres
Trustees of Haddo and Earl of Haddo: 7,047 acres
Nicol Brothers: 6,500 acres
The MacRobert Trust Estate: 6,500 acres
Kildrummy (Jersey) Ltd: 6,200 acres
Thomas Innes of Learney: 5,900 acres
Monymusk Land Co. and Monymusk Estate: 5,486 acres
Master of Forbes & Trusts: 10,400 acres
Trustees of the Cluny Estates: 5,000 acres
Captain David W. S. Buchan & Children's Trust: 4,935 acres

Andrew Salvesen: 4,600 acres
James R. Ingelby: 4,500 acres
Mrs Robert and C. I. R. Wolridge Gordon: 4,500 acres
Barra Trust & Straloch Trust: 4,250 acres
Bruce Urquhart: 4,200 acres
Alisdair J. Barlas: 8,400 acres

*Who Owns Scotland?*

Hans Depre: 3,950 acres
Mrs Isabel J. B. Sole: 3,800 acres
Pittodrie Estate: 9,700 acres
Cullerlie Trust: 6,000 acres
D. R. M. James-Duff & Trusts: 2,700 acres
Knockespock Estate Co.: 2,680 acres
R. L. O. Fyffe: 2,500 acres
L. A. and P. M. Gordon-Duff: 2,500 acres
Andrew Dingwall-Fordyce: 4,590 acres
William A. J. Davie: 4,400 acres
Meldrum Estate: 4,400 acres
Royal Society for the Protection of Birds: 2,029 acres
Peter, Sarah, and Richard Guthrie: 2,028 acres
Trustees of John Anderson: 2,000 acres
Udny and Dudwick Estates: 2,000 acres
Aboyne Castle Estate Trustees: 2,000 acres
Andrew E. H. Bradford: 2,000 acres
Trustees of Lt. Col. Forbes: 6,000 acres
C. R. Ratcliffe & family: 1,800 acres
Craigmyle Estates Ltd: 1,800 acres
Usborne & Son (London) Ltd: 1,700 acres

Trustees of James Allan: 1,700 acres
Sluie Estate Trust: 1,700 acres
C. E. I. Harding: 1,500 acres
Hamish C. McLean: 1,500 acres
James C. A. and Alexander J. A. Burnett: 1,500 acres
William K. A. J. Chambers Hunter: 1,500 acres
I. M. Smith: 1,500 acres
Craigie Farm Estates: 1,500 acres
Trustees of Alfred E. Jones: 4,500 acres
Crown Trust Fund: 1,401 acres
ON MARKET: 1,391 acres
ON MARKET: 1,317 acres

*Who Owns Scotland?*

Corsindae & Fetternear Farms: 1,300 acres
Crannach Management Group: 1,261 acres
Alistair J. Lilburn: 1,250 acres
M. Calvert: 2,500 acres
A. Howie: 2,400 acres
Stephen and Susan Mackie: 1,160 acres
ON MARKET: 1,103 acres
Herbst Peat and Energy (Scotland): 1,047 acres
Jolyon V. Robinson and S. W. Robinson: 1,030 acres
ON MARKET: 1,012 acres
Alassandro Muratori: 1,000 acres
Andrew D. Tennant: 1,100 acres
The Executors and D. M. Godsman and N. M. Godsman: 1,000 acres
Trustees of David W. Stewart: 1,000 acres
Electricity Supply Nominees: 1,000 acres

Mrs Flora M. M. Williams: 1,000 acres
ON MARKET: 1,000 acres
Geordie Burnett-Stuart: 1,000 acres
Irene Bell Tawse: 1,000 acres
Mrs D. A. Stancioff: 1,000 acres
Trustees of Ardhuncart Estate: 5,000 acres
Thomas Ingleby: 1,000 acres
Malcolm Hay: 800 acres
Co-op Wholesale Society Ltd: 550 acres
Captain John Hay of Delgatie: 500 acres

Total: 685,124 acres
Aberdeenshire Land Area: 1,261,333 acres
Area of county accounted for: 54.3 %

Alastair MacLennan
**1998**

Information sourced from *Who Owns Scotland?* by Andy Wightman (Canongate, 1996). These names were broadcast from Street Level gallery on King Street (Glasgow). Police responded to complaints from local shop keepers and only allowed the performance to continue once the sound level was reduced.

# A Proposal

Ross Birrell
Glasgow

Dear Sir David Steel,

As part of Scotland's Year of the Artist 1 June 2000–31 May 2001, I propose a year long residency at the Scottish Parliament. I view this not so much as a 'residency' at the Scottish Parliament but as an 'occupancy' of the Parliament by an artist.

During this period of 'occupancy' I would not make an art object for display. Rather I would organise event-structured interventions into the physical and social fabric of the Parliament, which aim to engage all the communities of the parliament, including Janitors, Cleaners, Policemen, Administrative Staff, Journalists, and MSPs.

From October to December 2000 I propose to organise and run a seven-week 'Night Class in Utopia', open to all those who work in the Parliament. The Night Class would be taught by Dr. Kevin Francis (Lecturer in Politics, Department of Government, Strathclyde University) and held in the Central Debating Chamber. At the end of the course, each of the participants would be asked to write their vision of an ideal society. These would then be published along with other documentation of the class.

Music often speaks more directly to people than politics and from March–May 2001, the Central Debating Chamber would be taken over in the evening for a series of televised 'unplugged' concerts by young Scottish bands, such as Teenage Fanclub, Primal Scream, the Pastels, Belle and Sebastian, Mogwai, Life Without Buildings, the Beta Band, and Travis. This would bring popular youth culture right to the heart of a political environment which is often viewed as alienating and distant by young people.

Other projects and proposals will be developed throughout the year in response to the Parliament and unfolding political events.

Ross Birrell
August 2000

The Scottish
Parliament

**The Rt Hon Sir David Steel KBE MSP**
**The Presiding Officer**

／／ September 2000

Dear Mr Birrell

Thank you for your letter of 29 August 2000 regarding Scotland's Year of the Artist and your proposal for a residency at the Scottish Parliament.

I am conscious that you are disappointed by the outcome of our discussions with Scottish Cultural Enterprise. I am writing to reassure you that all the pertinent factors were considered when taking the decision on potential support of this scheme and its constituent proposals, including your own. The SPCB does not normally undertake direct discussions with external parties at its meetings but the relevant written submissions were fully examined.

We appreciated the creativity and willingness to be flexible encapsulated in your proposal. However committing to an ambitious project like this, even with maximum flexibility on both sides, is simply outwith the scope of the SPCB, its staff and accommodation at present. Our main purpose has to be to develop and operate our core parliamentary business areas, especially in these first years in existence. In both policy and implementation terms, this project does not fall within our current priorities and workload capacity.

As all the relevant information was available and fully considered by the SPCB, we cannot consider any appeal. I have consulted the relevant officers and am content that no verbal or written indication of any likely support was given, either to Scottish Cultural Enterprise (SCE) or to yourself, at any point in the discussion process. Also I am informed that you were consistently advised that your project could only be considered as part of the overall SCE scheme. I must advise you that our decision on this project should be regarded as final therefore.

I am hopeful that we may have the capacity for a wider range of activities in the future when we move to our permanent accommodation at Holyrood. With this is mind, I have passed details of Scottish Cultural Enterprise to the relevant officers for consideration, e.g. when reviewing the art strategy for the Holyrood building.

Once again, please do rest assured that our decision was based on full deliberation of all the appropriate information and, of course, upon a sound assessment of our current capacity to participate in partnership schemes.

**David Steel**

After the rejection of this proposal Birrell organised a decentralised residency project holding site-specific public dialogues across Scotland.

# Under Darkness, Between Shadows

As the sun goes down on any city we look to light and electricity to get some sense of scale, architecture and the social behaviour of the place. This can be read as a practical necessity or as a metaphor. Different cities have different levels of light, and this is not only in respect of population numbers or traffic control. For instance, a small city like Belfast is brighter than Glasgow, for reasons of security. Urban behaviour is directly related to light levels: it is interesting to note that during the trade union strikes of the mid-1970s, when people were asked to 'switch off something NOW', the country experienced a baby-boom. So, even while the metaphor of darkness is associated with death, the reality is that 'the dark' only encourages the social behaviour that stimulates life.

As we leave the 1990s and begin to adapt to life in the twenty-first century, there are fewer people around who can remember a time when darkness enveloped the city (the winters of discontent in the 1970s, but more importantly the years 1942–45, under threat of aerial bombardment). Most of us can only relate to each other and the buildings we inhabit with the help of electric light. If we are deprived of this element, then we start to behave and communicate differently and negotiate the space of the city as a new experience.

'Under Darkness, Between Shadows' is a proposal to cut off all light in an area of Glasgow for one hour, at a time and date to be specified. The area of darkness should be one square mile. When viewed from above, this would be seen as a perfect black square cutting into the 'fabric' of the city.

The darkness would extend to all domestic lights, streetlamps and other devices using electricity for light in the area of the square mile. The darkness should fall immediately 'on the flick of a switch' and remain for one hour. At the end of this time, the city lights should begin to re-appear slowly, almost one at a time, until the area is fully illuminated.

Douglas Gordon
**2000**

# Acknowledgements

Thanks are due to the following copyright holders for permission to reproduce the works in this collection. While every effort has been made to trace and credit copyright holders, the Publishers will be glad to rectify any oversights in any future editions.

PETER ARNOTT & PETER MULLAN: 'Beechgrove Garden Festival', from *Workers City*, first published by Clydeside Press, Glasgow, 1988. BELTANE: Photograph © by Marius Alexander, 1997. MARK BOYLE: Still from 16mm film 'DIG' by David Naden Associates; 'Judge, Jury . . .' and extract, from *Journey to the Surface of the Earth*, edition hansjörg mayer, 1970, reproduced courtesy of the Boyle family. TOM BUCHAN: 'Scotland the Wee' first published in *Lines Review* no. 22, 1966; 'Letter from a Partisan' from *Poems 1969–1972*, The Poni Press, Edinburgh, 1972. RICHARD DEMARCO: 'Royal Botanical Gardens', 'Map of Scotland', photos by Robert LeBeck; 'Beuys & Demarco', 'STRATEGY:GET ARTS', 'Banana Trap Dinner', 'Fish Net', photos by George Oliver courtesy of Cordelia Oliver; all other photos by Richard Demarco reproduced courtesy of the Demarco European Art Foundation (DEAF). IAN HAMILTON FINLAY: *Ocean Stripe 5*, published by Tarasque Press, 1967; interview extract from 'Spartan Defence: Ian Hamilton Finlay in conversation with Peter Hill', Studio International Vol. 196, No. 1004, 1984. ALISON FLETT: 'Uniform Feelings', from *Clocktower Press No. 8* reprinted courtesy of Jonathan Cape © 1993. ALASDAIR GRAY: extract from 'Something Leather' © Alasdair Gray 1990, used by permission of Random House Inc. R. D. LAING: book cover design by Jay J. Smith, photo John Haynes, used by permission of Taylor & Francis Books Ltd. JOHN LATHAM: 'Niddrie Woman' reproduced courtesy of Lisson Gallery, London. TOM LEONARD: 'Shorter Catechism on the Gulf War' reprinted courtesy of AK Press, Edinburgh.

MARY MCCARTHY: extract from *The Correspondence of Hannah Arendt & Mary McCarthy* reprinted courtesy of Harcourt Brace & Co, Orlando,. TOM MCGRATH: 'Riverside Interview' reprinted courtesy of Gavin Selerie, Binnacle Press, © 1983. CHARLES MAROWITZ: 'Happening' from *New Writers 4*, Calder Publishers, London, © 1963. EDWIN MORGAN: 'The Angries', from a translation of Yevteshenko's poem, and 'Starryveldt', reprinted courtesy of Carcanet, Manchester, © 1965. GRANT MORRISON: extract from 'The Invisibles' reproduced courtesy of DC Comics, © New York 1994. PURE: photos by Spice, Scottie and friends, 1990–2000. ALAN RIDDELL: 'Revolver II', reproduced courtesy of Calder Publishers, London, © John Calder & Alan Riddel/Ann Barr, 1972. ALEXANDER TROCCHI: book cover and extract from 'Cain's Book' reproduced courtesy of Calder Publishers, London, © 1966. VARIANT: cover of issue 6, © Malcolm Dickson & Lorna Waite, 1988. KENNETH WHITE: *Letters from Gourgounel*, reproduced courtesy of Jonathan Cape, London © Kenneth White & Jonathan Cape 1966. IAN WILSON: 'Oral Communication' from *Six Years: The Dematerialization of the Art Object from 1966 to 1972*, Lucy R Lippard, © 1973, reprinted courtesy of the University of California Press.

# pocketbooks

our

scheme

is

only

a

sketch[1]

1. Plato, *The Laws*, Book Six

David Bellingham
From *Four Propositions* (WAX366)
**2000**